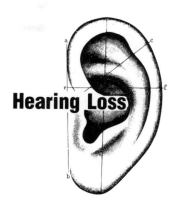

Hearing Loss

BY KARIN N. MANGO

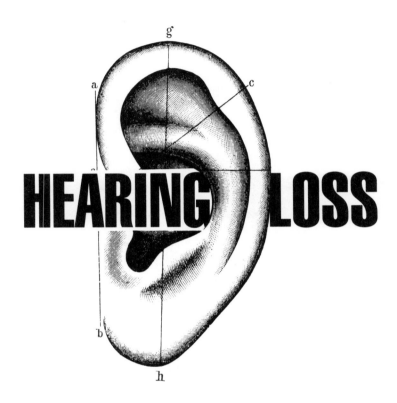

HEARING LOSS

Franklin Watts

New York ● London ● Toronto ● Sydney
A Venture Book   1991

Photographs courtesy of: Photo Researchers: p. 17; Gallaudet University, Mr. Chun Louie: pp. 28, 30, 59, 75 (reprinted from *Discovering Sign Language* by Greene and Dicker, Gallaudet University Press); National Association of the Deaf: p. 38; Lexington School for the Deaf: pp. 64, 112; New York League for the Hard of Hearing: p. 97; American Speech-Language-Hearing Association: pp. 105, 107 (all reprinted from *How to Buy a Hearing Aid*); National Captioning Institute/ABC: p. 114; Red Acre Farm Hearing Dog Center: pp. 121, 124; Self Help for Hard of Hearing People, Inc.: p. 131.

Library of Congress Cataloging-in-Publication Data

Mango, Karin N.
Hearing loss / by Karin N. Mango.
p.   cm. — (A Venture book)
Includes bibliographical references and index.
Summary: Describes the conditions and varying degrees of hearing loss and deafness, and discusses methods by which the hearing-impaired can communicate with others.
ISBN 0-531-12519-X
1. Deafness—Juvenile literature.   2. Deaf—Juvenile literature.
3. Deaf—Means of communication—Juvenile literature.   [1. Deaf.]
I. Title.
RF291.37.M36   1991
617.8—dc20   90-19746 CIP AC

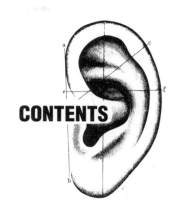

CONTENTS

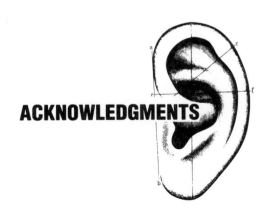

ACKNOWLEDGMENTS

The author would like to thank the following people and organizations for their invaluable help and their unstintingly given time:

The New York League for the Hard of Hearing, especially Ruth Green, MA, CRC, Jane Madell, Ph.D., Diane Brackett, Ph.D., Ellen Pfeffer, MA, CCC-A, Frida Grauer, BA, MLS, and Esther Beckoff, MA, CCC-SLP. The charts on pages 97–102 are used by permission of the League.

Lexington School for the Deaf, especially Adrianne Robins, supervisor, reading and writing program; Terri Donaldson, junior high teacher, and her class; Ronni Hollander, fifth grade teacher, and her class; and Denise O'Brien, Ph.D., Director, Lexington Hearing and Speech Center.

Red Acre Farm Hearing Dog Center, especially Ellen Terryberry, MA, program director, Dana Crevling, MA, trainer, and Hatti, demonstration dog; and for permission to quote the material on pages 123 and 125.

Self Help for Hard of Hearing People, Inc., for permission to use the material on page 131.

Special thanks to Renata Scheder, Estelle Stein, and Hannah Merker. And Tony.

7

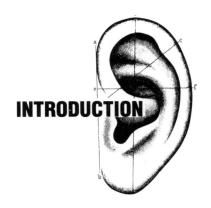

INTRODUCTION

Rose and Martin Robertson are talking about the movie they have just seen at the club, a comedy with closed captions. They face each other, animatedly moving their hands and fingers. Their expressions change to match their hand movements. They do not speak; they are communicating by signing. American Sign Language is their native language.

In a junior high school classroom, eight students are discussing a Sherlock Holmes story with their teacher. Most of them are using FM systems to follow more easily what the teacher is saying through the microphone. The kids have a lot to say, and the atmosphere is lively.

Mr. Walters has had good health throughout his life. He is sixty-five now and feels pretty good. But recently he has been noticing that people seem to speak less clearly. He has to turn the radio and TV volume higher to understand everything. And when there are more than a couple of people in a group, he can't follow the conversation very well. He knows there is nothing wrong with his health or his mind. It must be something else.

9

These are different people in different situations. You might think there is no connection between them. But there is a common thread. All these people have some degree of hearing loss.

The signing couple communicating visually have been profoundly deaf from birth and grew up as part of the deaf community. The kids in the classroom have hearing losses ranging from moderate and severe to profound. They use hearing aids enhanced by technological devices; combining these with lipreading and their residual hearing they are learning to function in the hearing world around them. Mr. Walters is beginning to be hard of hearing, a frequent accompaniment to getting older. He will probably soon get a hearing evaluation and a hearing aid. He will have to adjust to a new life-style after a lifetime of normal hearing.

All these people have lesser or greater difficulty in coping with the world of sound.

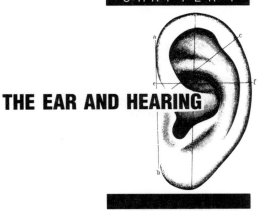

CHAPTER 1

THE EAR AND HEARING

It is difficult to imagine a world without sound. Try it: Sit in a quiet room alone, with the doors and windows closed. Plug your ears with cotton and put your hands over them. Listen. Silence? Not really, even then. Although sound is considerably dimmed, you know what is going on out there and you can still faintly hear it—traffic in the street, the television next door, or footsteps in the house. You can hear yourself take a deep breath, sneeze, and shift position. Your ears are still attuned to sound.

Or try this: Turn on the television set, but turn off the sound. Tune in to a program—any program—and try to make sense of what everyone is saying without being able to hear any of the words, any of the sounds. Did you get anything at all? It is very difficult to understand without sound.

What is meant by sound? Sound is a form of energy. All kinds of energy travel great distances and some, like light and electricity, travel incredibly fast. Sound moves relatively slowly. For example, you can see the brilliant fireworks display a second or two before you hear the bangs. But even "relatively slowly" is pretty fast. Sound travels at 760 miles (1216 km) per hour (known as Mach 1 after Ernst Mach, an Austrian physicist and philosopher). To

11

give you an idea of how fast that is, very few planes go faster. When they do, like the supersonic Concorde, they are said to break the sound barrier. Sound actually travels fastest through solids like metal or wood; slower through liquids, and most slowly through gases like those making up air. It cannot pass through a vacuum.

Sound is produced when something—a trumpet, for example—causes vibrations in the air or other medium. The trumpet makes molecules of air vibrate. This causes a disturbance in the surrounding air as the molecules strike those molecules nearest them and they in turn strike others. The disturbance radiates outward, forcing the molecules close together, then spreading them apart in "S" curves like waves—we call them sound waves. If you could see a sound wave it would look something like this:

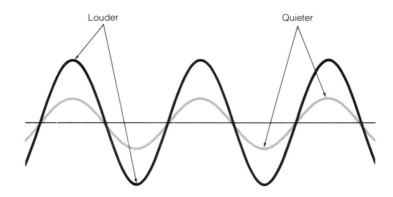

The distance between the crest (high point) and trough (low point) of the wave indicates the loudness of the sound. Loudness, or volume, is measured in *bels* (after Alexander Graham Bell, 1847–1922, the inventor of the telephone). For precise measuring we more often use *decibels* (dB). A decibel is one-tenth of a bel. Look at the table for an idea

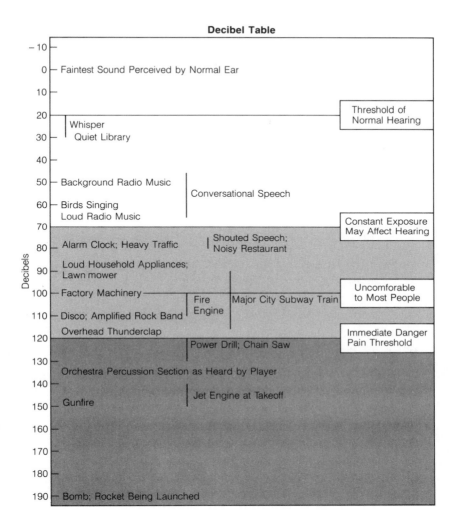

Decibel Table

Decibels			
−10			
0	Faintest Sound Perceived by Normal Ear		
10			
20			Threshold of Normal Hearing
30	Whisper / Quiet Library		
40			
50	Background Radio Music	Conversational Speech	
60	Birds Singing / Loud Radio Music		
70			Constant Exposure May Affect Hearing
80	Alarm Clock; Heavy Traffic	Shouted Speech; Noisy Restaurant	
90	Loud Household Appliances; Lawn mower		
100	Factory Machinery	Fire Engine · Major City Subway Train	Uncomforable to Most People
110	Disco; Amplified Rock Band		
120	Overhead Thunderclap		Immediate Danger Pain Threshold
130	Orchestra Percussion Section as Heard by Player	Power Drill; Chain Saw	
140		Jet Engine at Takeoff	
150	Gunfire		
160			
170			
180			
190	Bomb; Rocket Being Launched		

of the relative loudness or softness of different sounds. Bels work like this: A sound measuring one bel (ten decibels) more than another is ten times as intense. A sound two bels (20 decibels) more will be one hundred times as intense, and so on. Each addition of 10 decibels doubles

13

the energy. For example, background music from a radio is about 50 decibels. An amplified rock band, at 110 decibels, is potentially a million times as intense!

The higher the bel/decibel level, the higher the intensity of the sound, and the louder it will be. And the lower the bel/decibel level, the lower the intensity of the sound, and the softer it will be. Loudness also varies depending on the frequency (see below). And, of course, one person's "loud" isn't necessarily another's; to a certain extent it is subjective.

Sound is also measured by the distance between the crests of the waves, which is called, appropriately, the *wavelength*. The number of sound wave cycles per second (cps or hertz/hz) produced by a trumpet or other sound is the *frequency* or *pitch*. (The "hertz" measurement is named in honor of the German physicist Heinrich Rudolf Hertz, 1857–1894.)

People normally can respond through hearing to a range of about 20 to 20,000 cycles per second/hertz. The easiest range for human hearing is 500 to 4000 cps/hz, and most speech sounds are between 500 and 2000 cps/hz. High-frequency sounds are high in pitch; low-frequency ones are low in pitch. Think of the way a piano keyboard works; lower-pitched notes are in the bass at the left; higher-pitched notes in the treble at the right. Middle C on the piano is 256 hz. Men's voices are generally lower in pitch; women's and children's are higher. The very lowest notes in the hertz range can be felt rather than heard, and loud noises at the extreme ends of the range are actually painful as well as dangerous for the ears.

Two sounds may have the same intensity and pitch and yet "sound" quite different—an oboe and a cello, for example. The reason for this is that the sound waves each instrument produces vary in quality or *timbre*. Timbre depends on the number and intensity of the subsidiary tones produced by the vibrating instrument and that in turn depends on the essential character of the instrument itself.

14

Hertz and decibel measurements are the basis for the audiogram in a hearing test, as you will see in chapter 9.

Hearing is perceiving sound. And ears are for hearing. That seems obvious, but, while you can see ears, you can't see hearing. The parts of the ear where hearing takes place are deep inside the head. They are very complex. If they were human-made, they would be miracles of technology. They are, anyway! The drawing gives you some idea of the complexity of the human ear.

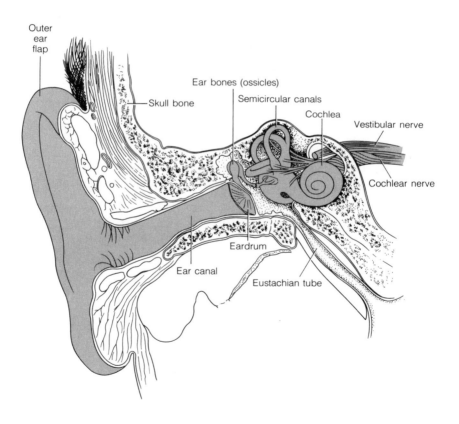

The outer ear, the part of the ear you can see, is the least interesting; it simply acts as a funnel for sound. Animals that rely primarily on sound usually have large, funneling ears that can turn toward the source of the sound for better reception. Dogs, horses, and rabbits are good examples. Dogs have highly sensitive hearing; they can hear ultrasonic sounds beyond human range. Bats' ears are even more sensitive: Their squeaks, which bounce back to them during echolocation, can reach 50,000 hz.

Cats also have extremely sensitive hearing, enabling them to respond to high-pitched sounds such as a mouse's squeak or a kitten's meow, often well above the limits of human hearing. An oddity among cats is the genetic (hereditary) deafness that often occurs in white cats with blue eyes. The gene causing the deafness also affects eye and coat color to varying degrees. This deafness is caused by defective development of the inner ear or degeneration of the cochlea which can occur in the first days after birth. In white cats with one blue eye and one gold or brown eye, often only the ear on the blue-eyed side is deaf.

Praying mantises, long thought to be deaf, have a single ultrasonic hearing structure in the center of their bellies. And turtles hear by bone conduction through their shells which are live bone.

Sound is around us all the time. We hear whether we are aware of it or not. This is how hearing works:

THE OUTER EAR

Sound is collected in the *pinna,* the flap-shaped part of the ear you can see, and funneled into the *ear canal.* This is a passage about an inch long lined with delicate skin that is covered with fine hairs. The skin secretes *cerumen* (ear wax), which traps dirt and prevents it from reaching the eardrum at the end of the canal.

Dogs can hear sounds that
have too high a pitch for
human beings to hear.

The *eardrum,* or tympanic membrane, is a thin, oval membrane about half-an-inch high. It stretches across the inner end of the ear canal, like the skin of a drum, and covers the entrance to the middle ear. It is tough, but can be perforated if something sharp is pushed into the ear. Never put anything smaller than your elbow into your ear!

Energy from the sound waves entering the ear canal makes the eardrum vibrate.

THE MIDDLE EAR

The middle ear is basically an amplifier. It is a narrow space, about one-eighth of an inch wide and three-quarters of an inch high. The "attic" area contains the greater part of the "works." Attached to the inner side of the eardrum is the first of the three tiny bones, *ossicles,* that conduct vibrations to the inner ear. Because of their shapes they are called the *malleus,* or hammer (the largest), the *incus,* or anvil, and the *stapes,* or stirrup. The stapes is the smallest bone in the body, smaller than a small kernel of corn. These bones are attached to each other by ligaments. Joined together like the cab and trailer of a truck, they move as one unit in the air space of the middle ear, increasing the vibrations of the eardrum and sending them to the inner ear. The stapes is attached by its base to the membrane of the back wall of the cavity called the *oval window.* This separates the middle ear from the inner ear and transmits vibrations. The oval window is backed by the *round window.* The round window moves out when the oval window is pushed into the inner ear by the base of the stapes, equalizing the pressure. The oval window leads to the inner ear.

The middle ear also contains a safety device. At the lower end, the *Eustachian tube* leads to the back of the nose and throat, conveying air to the middle ear and equalizing the air pressure on both sides of the eardrum. Too much pressure on either side could damage the eardrum. You notice the effect of too much pressure on one side of the eardrum when you go up or down in an airplane: your ears "pop." You can help equalize the air pressure by yawning or swallowing; this forces air through the Eustachian tube.

The main work of hearing is done in the inner ear.

THE INNER EAR

The inner ear occupies a cavity in the skull and is filled with fluid. The cavity contains the *cochlea*, the *semicircular canals*, and the ends of the hearing, or *auditory*, nerve.

Vibrations coming through the oval window start a wave in the fluid filling the cochlea. The bony cochlea, Latin for "snail" because it is coiled like a snail shell, contains three separate, liquid-filled ducts. The middle one, the cochlear duct, contains the organ of Corti, a thin membrane that goes the length of the cochlea and is the part of the ear where sound is directly perceived. This is where the sound vibrations are registered and converted to nervous impulses going to the brain.

The waves in the cochlea agitate the *basilar membrane* suspended in the center (on which the organ of Corti rests), setting in motion the 20,000 hairlike nerve fibers attached to sensory cells. These in turn are attached to the organ of Corti. They bend, swaying like reeds in a pond. Each of the hairs responds to pitch. Loud sounds make them move more than soft sounds. High-pitched sounds and low-pitched sounds make the hair cells in different areas move. This bending by sound waves stimulates the sensory hearing cells to send electrical impulses along the auditory nerve for processing and decoding into meaning.

Inside the brain the impulses go through incredibly fast and very complicated processes before you understand what you are hearing. The brain also "compares notes" with what is coming in from the other ear, filters out unwanted "noise" signals, and allows you to know from which direction the sound is coming. You are then conscious of hearing—and most of the time know what it is you are hearing. An adult can recognize about 500,000 different sounds. A sound entering the brain is checked against the person's memory. If it is in the memory, the brain takes no action. If the sound is new it is added to the stored collection.

The *semicircular canals,* three loop-shaped tubes also housed in the inner ear, are not involved with hearing. Their job is to help you keep your balance.

Your ears and brain are constantly and continuously at work making sense of your environment—locating, assessing, warning, and reassuring—and enabling you to communicate. A normal-hearing person hears all the time, effortlessly—in fact, quite passively. It is only when hearing is damaged in some way that you have to work at it. Then you have to become an active participant in your own listening and hearing.

The rest of this book will tell you how hearing can be damaged or lost and how people communicate and learn throughout their lives in spite of hearing loss. You will also learn how to protect your hearing so that you can always use all five of your senses.

CHAPTER 2

HEARING LOSS—WHAT IT IS AND HOW IT HAPPENS

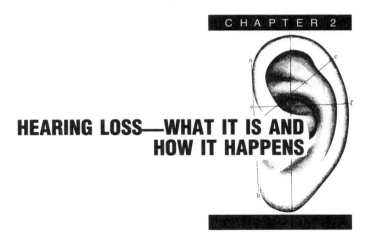

Let's go back for a moment to the people discussed in the introduction to this book. Would you describe them as deaf? Deafened? Hard of hearing? Hearing impaired? One or all of these? There are many definitions of hearing loss, and they are not precise, just as there is no strict division between the varying degrees of hearing loss. One rule-of-thumb definition was given by a teacher of lipreading to her class: "If you have your eyes closed and therefore can't communicate, I would consider you deaf."

Two million people in the United States cannot hear speech or understand language through their ears, with or without the use of hearing aids. They process language with their eyes. Between eighteen and twenty-one million people in this country have some degree of hearing impairment and communicate orally by speaking. A relatively small percentage use hearing aids and other assistive devices.

Speech is a physical process using many parts of the body including lips, tongue, vocal cords, and ears. *Language* enables the mind to shape thoughts, ideas, and feelings and to communicate them to other people in a systematic way. Language is enhanced by learning and experience.

21

DEGREES OF HEARING LOSS

The amount of hearing loss can be expressed in decibel levels. Ninety decibels and higher means that the person can't hear sounds softer than 90 decibels and is therefore profoundly hearing impaired, or deaf. Hearing aids will not be of much, if any, help. Few people are so deaf that they can literally hear nothing. Many profoundly deaf people sense vibrations that give some clues to sound. Lower frequencies may be perceived. Other profoundly deaf people can hear speech with the help of considerable amplification.

Someone who can only hear at decibel levels of 70 to 90 and above is considered to have a severe hearing loss and, without aids, can only hear very loud speech close to the ear, and then not clearly. Hearing aids will be of some help.

A hard-of-hearing person is someone whose sense of hearing is defective, with a loss ranging from mild (25 to 40 decibels) to moderate (40 to 70). Hard-of-hearing people can usually be helped by hearing aids, lipreading/speechreading, and assistive devices like amplified telephones. They function in the hearing world with varying degrees of success. In general, more men than women are hard of hearing. As people age, however, more women are hard of hearing because they tend to live longer. We will be talking about hard-of-hearing people in detail later on; the first half of this book will focus on deaf people.

PRELINGUAL DEAFNESS

People who are born deaf or who become deaf before they have had a chance to learn language as young children, up to the age of three or so, are called *congenitally* or *prelingually* deaf (from the Latin "pre-lingua," meaning "before language''). Those with deaf parents mostly use manual communication—sign language—and generally feel comfortable with themselves and are usually part of the deaf community. They have a culture and a language—predominantly American Sign Language (ASL)—in common. Those with hearing parents, the vast majority of deaf people, may have more difficulty both with their identity and with learning language since they are different from their parents and the surrounding hearing culture.

POSTLINGUAL DEAFNESS

People who become deaf after they have learned to speak are called *adventitiously* or *postlingually* deaf (''post'' is Latin for after); they have *acquired* deafness. Postlingually deaf people, if deafened after age twelve or so, usually remain in the hearing world they were born into, and where they have had their life experience. They usually try to remain oral but may also learn sign language. One of their challenges is to retain a good speaking voice once they can no longer hear themselves speak. They have a particularly rough burden to bear. Those born deaf do not know normal sound. Those who have known it and are deprived of it know what they have lost. Again, try to imagine a world without the sounds you love and are familiar with. It is difficult to say which is the greater trauma: Sudden deafness or its gradual onset.

People who have lost their hearing later in life due to disease, injury, noise, and/or degeneration because of aging are just as deaf as congenitally deaf people, but have a hearing person's view of life. It is not only a physical condition; they often have difficulty finding a niche. They seem to belong neither to the world of the hearing nor to that of the deaf.

Postlingually deafened children are encouraged to be as oral as possible, using the spoken word as their chief means of communication so they can be as much a part of the larger hearing world as possible. The degree of success depends on the amount of residual, or remaining, hearing a child has and whether the stress of trying to be oral is too great. In any event, a profoundly deaf child should learn sign language.

"Hearing impairment" is the umbrella term used to include all types of hearing loss. A gray area exists between those who cannot hear even with hearing aids and those who can only hear with them. Hearing loss is so individual that every hearing-impaired person's loss is unique. What is not unique is the isolation that hearing loss can impose on people because of the difficulty of communicating with others. Inability to function in the hearing world can have major effects on personality and on a person's position and ambitions in society. The hearing-impaired person has to work very hard to achieve what hearing people take for granted.

CAUSES OF DEAFNESS

There are many different causes of deafness. Some occur before a baby is born. A child can inherit deafness. Or a mother who has rubella (German measles) or some other viral infection while she is pregnant can have a deaf or otherwise handicapped child. A premature baby, born before the full nine months of development, or a full-term baby experiencing a difficult birth with accompanying lack of oxygen, has a possibility of being deaf. After birth, a child can have illnesses that can result in hearing loss. Meningitis, otitis media (middle ear infection), mumps, measles, and high fevers are the most potentially damaging of such illnesses. Injuries, ototoxic (harmful to the ears) drugs, and very loud or constant noise can deafen a person.

24

While the numbers of hearing-impaired people are increasing in general, a drop has occurred in some types of cases because antibiotics help keep down the high fevers accompanying certain diseases that used to cause inner ear nerve destruction.

People who are deaf have had difficulty being accepted by the hearing world. They have suffered discrimination, hostility, and patronizing attitudes from many hearing people just because they lack a sense of hearing, and hearing people have difficulty understanding what that means. Things are, however, changing in many ways—in public attitudes, acceptability, equality, and civil rights. Hearing-impaired people, from hard of hearing to deaf, are changing, too. They are now learning how to take their rightful places in the world.

CHAPTER 3

HEARING LOSS IN HISTORY

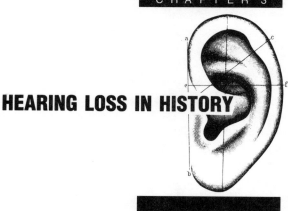

"The baby is deaf. We will have to drown it in the river."

Maybe the actual words were less harsh, but in ancient times a child discovered to be handicapped, and that included being deaf, was not allowed to survive.

It was assumed that a defect in the mind caused deafness and lack of speech. People then did not understand that it was anatomy or physiology that prevented a person from hearing, and as a result the person could not learn how to speak. Aristotle said the deaf were "incapable of reason," that is, of reasoned thinking.

Through many centuries that followed, the deaf, although permitted to live, were considered impossible to educate, and their disability was viewed as a punishment from God. "Medical" treatment was based on ignorance and, though often imaginative, was useless. A thirteenth century "remedy," for example, prescribed the "heart of a weasel, dried, and placed with wax in the ear." Another remedy, not only useless but painful, was to pour hot oil into the ears.

We know very little about deaf people in early times, but it is clear that they led hard, isolated lives with little access to communication.

There were the occasional flashes of light. One was Girolamo Cardano (1501–1576), an Italian physician, mathematician, and astrologer who was an exceptional thinker even in the context of the Renaissance. He understood that mental ability was not connected to one's ears. Being deaf should not prevent a person from acquiring language skills, though not necessarily speech.

Pedro Ponce de Leon (ca. 1520–1584), a Spanish Benedictine monk, was able to teach deaf students to speak, write, and use a kind of sign language. This method, or one very similar to it, was used about seventy years later by another Spaniard, Juan Pablo Bonet, who published the first book on the education of the deaf.

Several other books were published in the seventeenth century describing their authors' approaches to teaching speech and manual communication. They all concentrated on what the deaf could not do—speak—and ignored the other aspects of their lives. The aim, naturally, was to enable people to join the hearing world and live successfully in it.

It was not until the mid-eighteenth century, however, that schools for the deaf were founded. Two opposing philosophies immediately became apparent, and a controversy began that has not been solved even today. The controversy centered on which was the most effective method of communication and therefore education: Manual communication/sign language or oral communication/speech and lipreading, also called speechreading.

The first organized attempts to educate the deaf were made by Samuel Heinicke (1729–1790), a German, and the Abbé Charles Michel de L'Epée (1712–1789), a Frenchman. Heinicke started the first school to teach a mainly oral method of communication in 1778. L'Epée also founded a school, funding it with his own money and running it with great devotion to his students. He used sign language as his main teaching method. Like Heinicke, L'Epée was a hearing person. He added to the sign language he watched his students using among themselves. Of course his additions and changes were based on his

27

*Abbé de L'Epée not only founded one
of the first schools for the deaf,
but was the first to use sign language
as the means of communication and
education at the school.*

own native French. He developed what was essentially a signed version of spoken French. The Abbé is honored by the deaf community because he opened the door to its preferred mode of communication, sign language. His successor, the Abbé Roche Ambroise Sicard, was a brilliant teacher and passed on L'Epée's methods to an American, Reverend Thomas Hopkins Gallaudet (1787–1851), who brought them back to America early in the nineteenth century.

In 1816, Gallaudet had gone to Europe to learn what methods were being used there to educate the deaf. He went first to Britain to meet John Braidwood, who had started a school for the deaf in Edinburgh and used the oral method. Braidwood attached too many strings to his permission for Gallaudet to observe his methods, so Gallaudet looked elsewhere. But he had had time to see that the results of oral training were not particularly good. He was welcomed at Sicard's school in Paris, where he learned the methods and the combination of natural sign language and signed French that L'Epée had used. Gallaudet brought this language—and Sicard's best teacher, the deaf Laurent Clerc (with Sicard's blessing)—back to America.

By the next year, Gallaudet and Clerc were already starting their school, the first American school for the deaf, in Hartford, Connecticut. It had a typical nineteenth-century name of Asylum for the Education and Instruction of Deaf and Dumb Persons. It is now called the American School for the Deaf. Clerc must have felt comfortable at the school; he taught there for forty years.

Before Gallaudet started using the French-based sign language in his school, deaf people in America, as elsewhere, had communicated with one another in a variety of home-created signs. However, there were comparatively few deaf people, and they were scattered over the country with little mutual contact. An unusual cluster lived on Martha's Vineyard, an island off the coast of Massachusetts. An atypically high number of deaf people were concentrated there because of isolation, intermarriage, and large

29

*Thomas Gallaudet started the first
American school for the deaf.
Gallaudet respected the desire of
the deaf to use sign language
as their main means of communication.*

families with deaf children. Starting in the seventeenth century, so many deaf inhabitants had created and handed down a sign language that the hearing inhabitants were bilingual in speech and sign. This is perhaps a unique instance of sign language being taken completely for granted.

Gallaudet's school became a focus for deaf people, encouraging a community of the deaf to grow. They brought their own sign communication with them. Gallaudet had incorporated some of the schoolchildren's invented signs and gestures into the sign language he had learned in France. Now, as the deaf community developed, so did American Sign Language (ASL), spreading to other schools as they opened. About 60 percent of ASL signs are derived from the French sign language of Gallaudet's time.

Edward Miner Gallaudet, Thomas's son, went to Washington in 1857 at the age of twenty, accompanied by his deaf mother, to become superintendent of the Columbia Institution, a school for the deaf. Edward's ambition was to establish a college for the deaf. In 1864, President Lincoln signed a law allowing the institution to confer degrees, and in 1894 it became Gallaudet College, in honor of Thomas Hopkins Gallaudet. A stamp honoring him was issued in 1983. In 1986, the college was granted university status, and it is still the world's only liberal arts university for deaf students. Edward Miner Gallaudet, understanding that not all deaf people could be taught to speak, was a proponent of the combined method of speech and signing.

It was not, however, a unanimous opinion that sign language was the best method of communication. L'Epée and Heinicke had already been involved in a correspondence debating the merits of oral versus manual communication. In institutions where deaf teachers were in the majority, sign was the preferred method. Hearing educators were generally against sign; they believed the oral method produced better results. This was also the preferred method in Europe. Since the number of hearing educators outnumbered those who were deaf, and the vast majority

31

of concerned parents were hearing people with deaf children, new schools began to favor oralism.

Extra momentum was given to the oral method by Alexander Graham Bell, who strongly endorsed it. Bell, the inventor of the telephone, had a deaf mother and a deaf wife. He knew how to sign, but since his wife became successfully oral, Bell was led to believe that deaf people in general could be taught to speak.

The use of signs and fingerspelling was first disapproved of and then, after 1880, forbidden in schools. In 1880, the International Congress on Education of the Deaf met in Milan, Italy, and adopted a resolution that banned the use of sign language as a means of teaching deaf children. Hearing educators thought that allowing children to sign prevented them from acquiring speech, and therefore prevented them from learning the way other children did, putting them at a permanent disadvantage in a predominantly hearing world. ASL was not a proper language, these educators felt, and was a barrier to knowledge and to entry into the hearing world with its possibilities for a better life. Sign language forced those who did not speak into a ghetto life-style from which they could never escape.

The growing deaf community, on the other hand, wanted to keep sign language because it was the cohesive force in their community. They understood that speech and language were the keys to jobs, money, and success in the larger hearing world, and they therefore saw the material advantages of being bilingual. They were, however, fiercely against being forced into a mode of communication that was extremely difficult for them, and, additionally, having to compete with people for whom hearing and speech were instinctive. They also felt that a person who had failed in the hearing world might no longer fit into the world of the deaf.

Between 1880 and the 1960s, schools for the deaf used the oral method or they combined speech with some sign or fingerspelling. The proportion of deaf teachers to deaf students, about 50 percent in the mid-nineteenth century, dropped to half that by the beginning of the twentieth, and to around 12 percent by 1960. At the other end of the scale, the number of hearing teachers grew proportionally.

Until well into this century, most schools for the deaf were residential—boarding schools—because students came from all over the country, and transportation over great distances was difficult. The United States was, however, becoming more urbanized, and the population in general was growing. Day schools for the deaf increased in number, and children were not so cut off from their families and neighborhoods. A trend began that placed hearing-impaired children in regular schools. Those with normal speech and enough residual hearing to be helped by hearing aids, or with the memory of an earlier, hearing stage in their lives, kept up and graduated from school with some degree of success. Some deaf children, by struggling superhumanly, also coped. Those who could not fell behind and were labeled oral failures.

In the 1960s it was realized that ASL was a language in its own right and not merely pantomime or pictorial, the inferior and uneducated means of communication that many educators had thought. The focus during the 1960s on civil rights for the individual also helped produce a new respect for deaf people and their culture. Many people began to see that compelling a child to be totally oral did not necessarily mean that the system worked.

With the renewed interest in sign, a turning point was reached in communication and education theory. The Total Communication philosophy was developed in California in the early and mid-1960s and was supported by the National Association of the Deaf. It recommends using a variety of methods, including signing, speech, hearing aids, gestures, writing, and others—whatever gets the message across efficiently at a particular moment for a particular person. The emphasis is on sign, but the system is flexible, allowing for individual differences in the way people op-

33

erate. This reduces tension. It helps people acquire abstract concepts of language rather than concentrating on speech. At its best, Total Communication is meant to enhance self-confidence. A person's place in society should not be as a failed hearing person but as a successful deaf one.

In the 1960s and 1970s, Simultaneous Communication (Simcom) came into major use in schools. Simcom means using manual language and speech at the same time. Signing and speaking simultaneously were not new in the daily lives of many people, but many educators were becoming dissatisfied with the results of the purely oral method of education and saw the advantages of putting speech and sign together. Simcom is now used in most American schools for deaf children.

Another major turning point came in 1975 with the passage of Public Law 94–142, the Education for All Handicapped Children Act. This law stated that every handicapped American child was guaranteed ''a free, appropriate public education in the least restrictive environment,'' included due process safeguards, confidentiality, and nondiscriminatory testing and placement procedures. The law further mandated that each student was to have an Individualized Educational Program (IEP). This was to be fitted to the child's particular needs with input from the child's family as well as from teachers. The education was to be tailored to the child, not the child squeezed to fit the program. The IEP is reviewed annually.

The ''least restrictive environment'' rule encourages the education of handicapped children in a school program near their homes wherever possible and appropriate. This has most often meant ''mainstreaming'' them with regular students in the local public schools. While some aspects of mainstreaming had been started earlier in a much less ambitious way, PL 94–142 produced some special problems. The law does not refer specifically to deaf children: Deafness is one of the handicapping conditions included. Since the number of hearing-impaired students is comparatively small, educators are often unfamiliar with deafness in general and the necessary support services in particular, which are, in addition, expensive.

The law does not *require* the mainstreaming of handicapped students into regular classrooms; it tries to make possible the greatest participation in a normal educational setting feasible for a particular child. The concepts "mainstreaming" and "least restrictive environment" have had many different interpretations and have produced controversy. Ideally, putting them into practice should be based on the individual student's capabilities and potential in a particular educational system. It has been particularly hard for hearing-impaired children compared with other handicapped children. For many of them, mainstreaming has become the *most* restrictive environment. For a wheelchair-bound student, for example, once physical access is assured, the student should be able to learn in the normal way. The problems for hearing-impaired children center on the communication problems of hearing, understanding, speaking, and the social isolation these difficulties produce.

Mainstreaming works best, of course, for students with milder hearing losses. The more severe the impairment, the greater the need for specialized support services, and the greater the effort to be made by everyone, not least of all the student.

An increase in the number of hearing-impaired children because of a rubella epidemic in 1963 to 1965 made a large impact on the deaf population. Deafness is a fairly low-incidence disability; a comparatively small percentage of the population is hearing impaired. The large number of rubella-affected children, many of whom were multihandicapped, also had an impact on education, resulting in the development of more programs for children from infancy on.

The hearing impaired have taken a long time to start working for their legal rights.

35

The Architectural Barriers Act of 1968 started the drive toward a barrier-free environment for the disabled. While this meant physical changes like ramps for the wheelchair-bound, it also meant removal of *communication* barriers, like adjusting telephones so that hearing-impaired people could also use them.

Technology has played an increasingly large part in recent history, changing laws and enhancing many lives. Telephones and television are now more accessible, and hearing-impaired people can use various newly developed systems to participate in business meetings, the theater, and other events.

Discrimination in hiring has been another target of civil rights legislation. The purpose of the Rehabilitation Act of 1973 was to make sure that programs receiving federal money could be used by all disabled people. Major sections prohibit discrimination and require accessibility in employment, education and health, welfare, and social services.

Section 501 applies to federal government employment, requiring of each executive department and agency an affirmative action plan for hiring, placing and advancement of qualified handicapped people.

Section 504 prohibits discrimination against qualified handicapped people in any federally supported program or activity. Recipients of federal financial aid include most public institutions and some private ones and range from schools and hospitals to airports and cultural centers.

The Americans with Disabilities Act passed in 1990—called the "civil rights act for disabled Americans"—takes antidiscrimination into the private sector of business and commerce. It prohibits "discrimination on the basis of handicap in such areas as employment, housing, public accommodations, travel, communications, and activities of state and local governments."

For example, if a hearing-impaired electrician who is fully trained and able to carry out his duties is rejected for a job solely because he has a hearing loss, he is being discriminated against.

A National Institute on Deafness and Other Communication Disorders was created by law in 1988. This new institute, one of only thirteen at the National Institutes of Health in Bethesda, Maryland, focuses on research into the causes, ramifications, and possible solutions to hearing loss.

Laws like these are giving the hearing impaired a fairer place in the world and a better feeling about themselves. An event that bolstered this feeling considerably took place at Gallaudet University in 1988. The students rose up in a peaceful but determined protest against the appointment of a hearing person as the new president of the university. After a week of unified protest and discussion, a deaf president was appointed who would more accurately represent the university and affirm deaf people in all aspects of life. As a student leader put it: "We didn't just win our demands, we won respect—respect for our culture, our language, our rights as human beings."

Hearing impairment is a fact of life for millions of people. The hearing impaired are starting to have the courage to make it known; it's not something to be ashamed of. An International Symbol of the Deaf can now be seen at places like airports and railroad stations here and abroad, anywhere that communication might be difficult and help is available. In Britain, the Sympathetic Hearing Scheme uses the symbol more intensively to show where trained personnel are available at banks, post offices, stores, and other public places. Many people wear the symbol on a button to announce that they are hearing impaired in order to ease communication.

The hearing impaired have not all been anonymous. Many famous people are among them. Perhaps the most famous is Ludwig van Beethoven. He became so deaf that he could not even hear the tumultuous applause that greeted his conducting of his great Ninth Symphony. He had to be turned around in order to see it. He was not born deaf, and

*This International Symbol of the
Deaf helps the hearing impaired see
where help is available and helps
others realize that, for many,
deafness is a way of life.*

the agony he went through as he realized what was happening to his hearing is recorded in his "Heiligenstadt Testament," named for the suburb of Vienna where he wrote it. He wrote:

38

> **If on occasion I tried to ignore my disability,
> O how harshly was I defeated by the sad reality
> of my bad hearing and yet it was impossible for
> me to say to people, "Speak louder! Shout! Be-
> cause I am deaf." Alas how could it be possible
> for me to admit that I had an infirmity in the *one*
> sense that should really be more perfect in me
> than in others and indeed the one sense which I
> once did possess in the highest perfection.**

But occasionally Beethoven could also joke. Discussing the performance of a piece of music with another hearing-impaired composer, he suddenly began to laugh. "Two
deaf musicians trying to tell each other what to do!"

The Spanish artist Francisco Goya also became deaf.
A distinct difference can be seen in the works he painted
before and after he lost his hearing—from gay and charm-
ing to a darker, more graphic, and often savage view of
life.

Thomas Alva Edison, one of the world's greatest and
most prolific inventors, was deaf. Helen Keller who
triumphed over both deafness and blindness, became world-
renowned. Jonathan Swift, the great writer and satirist and
author of *Gulliver's Travels,* had a severe hearing loss.

Deaf athletes from all over the world compete in the
World Games for the Deaf. Stuntwoman Kitty O'Neil is
an Olympic-standard diver and has been called "the fastest
woman on earth" because she held a land speed record of
512.083 miles per hour in a rocket-powered car.

The National Theatre of the Deaf has brought sign to
a much larger audience and has shown it to be an art form.
The theatre has produced actresses like Phyllis Frelich. Both
she and Marlee Matlin became famous—and won awards—
for their performances in *Children of a Lesser God,* a play
and also a movie written by Mark Medoff about a deaf
woman, a hearing teacher, and a school for the deaf.

Deaf people have been successful in almost all spheres of life. There are deaf poets, artists, writers, musicians, lawyers, doctors . . .

The Rt. Hon. Jack Ashley, a member of Parliament in the British House of Commons, has proved that deafness need not be a bar even in a profession that relies almost totally on the spoken word. Ashley became deaf just before the era of assistive listening devices and, using whatever help he could find, as well as a thorough knowledge of lipreading, triumphed over an extraordinarily difficult situation.

History has only recently shown that a disability need not be the same as a handicap. A disability such as hearing loss becomes a handicap when environmental and social barriers prevent a person from functioning like others. Hearing-impaired people are learning to control their environments through more appropriate education; the use of hearing aids, assistive devices and/or sign language; and the natural acceptance of their peers. "Disabled" becomes "able." People are entitled to have their abilities, not their *dis*abilities, used as the touchstones of who they are. Dr. I. King Jordan, the president of Gallaudet University, has said, "The only thing deaf people can't do is hear!"

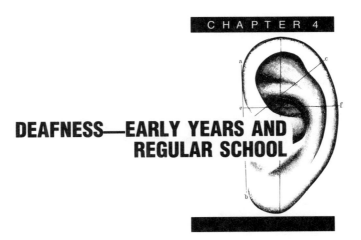

DEAFNESS—EARLY YEARS AND REGULAR SCHOOL

Alec's parents were very happy when he was born. He had his father's brown eyes and curly hair, though the hair was more a promise than a reality just then, and he evidently already had his mother's lively personality. He seemed like any other baby going through the early stages of development. But gradually his parents realized that something was not quite right. He was not responding, for example, when they said his name or when they clapped their hands out of his vision. Something was definitely wrong. They took him to their pediatrician, who recommended an ear doctor.

They were sad and upset to learn that Alec was not hearing properly. Careful and detailed audiological tests designed for the very young showed that he had a severe hearing loss. The news was broken to them gently, but their feelings of anger and depression, and the fear of the unknown future, lasted quite some time. They loved Alec and wanted him to have a happy, normal life. What should they do? How could they help him? They had no experience with hearing loss.

The most difficult part was accepting the situation. Once they could do that, they could turn for help. The audiological clinic at the hospital had a parent-child program to help children like Alec. He had only limited residual hear-

41

ing, but they felt he would be able to learn speech and language, the skills that normal-hearing children pick up instinctively through their ears.

Jean Piaget, a Swiss psychologist who lived from 1896 to 1980, showed in his theory of child development that a baby spends its time absorbing and learning about its immediate environment through its senses. A baby is hearing and listening all the time, gradually making sense of the world. In due course sounds become intelligible: people's voices, words, sentences, tones, meanings, laughter, crying, singing . . . The sounds of everyday life also take on meaning: a door closing, the cat meowing, traffic outside, the telephone ringing, siblings fighting, the rustle of a newspaper. . . .

Through interaction with their surroundings and immediate family, children also gradually learn to speak. First a baby babbles to itself, crying and making other vocal sounds. He hears himself, and he hears other people. In time the babbling changes to misspoken words, then proper words and sentences. The urge to speak, powerful in itself, is greatly stimulated by the surrounding world.

Piaget defined a sequence of stages in a child's development. At one and a half to two, for example, a child is ready to communicate verbally, and the hearing child starts to speak. By the age of two or three, a hearing child knows and uses hundreds of words and by the age of five has a good command of language. At five or six a child is usually ready to read. Young children learn a vast amount in their early years and accomplish much of this through hearing. To start with, they operate in a rather literal way: What they think is what they say and do. As they get older, they begin to think more conceptually and develop the language needed to express the abstract as well as the concrete.

The hearing-impaired child also tries to express himself, but he can't do it by listening, imitating, and experimenting with sound. If the amount of sound, intelligible or not, going into the ears has been limited, he may not be able to express himself verbally, and the frustration is enormous.

When Alec was little, he saw his parents' lips moving, but hardly any sounds were reaching his ears, so he couldn't give names to things in the normal way. He used gestures or pulled his mother to show what he wanted.

There are several roadblocks to acquiring speech. The later a child begins to learn, the harder it will be. The more severe the hearing loss, the more difficult it is to learn. Also of major importance is the age at which the hearing loss occurred, prelingually or postlingually, since the amount of language the child has prior to the hearing loss is crucial. Alec was very young, and he had a little residual hearing to offset the fact that he was prelingually hearing impaired. Early intervention and intensive speech training—as much as possible by the age of five or so—are essential. The sooner he could start learning to acquire speech and language, the easier it would be for him to cope with the challenges of growing up and going to school and to have the possibility of a full and fulfilling life in the hearing world. Some deaf children never acquire intelligible speech.

Alec's parents had to learn a great deal very fast about hearing impairment and the way speech and language develop. At the clinic Alec was fitted with hearing aids so that he could start learning to listen to all that was going on around him and start the long, slow process of learning to talk. With the hearing aids he could also hear his own voice a little and so could learn to make it sound more normal. He didn't want to wear the hearing aids, but his parents insisted. They didn't want any more precious time to be wasted. It took Alec some time to get used to the aids.

At the clinic, the speech-language pathologist used an FM auditory trainer with Alec to work on communication, developing and using residual hearing, and learning speech

43

and speechreading in the best conditions. The speaker's voice went through a microphone close to her mouth and a transmitter. Alec received the sound through a magnetic coil in his hearing aids. The FM system provided clear sound without distracting background noise. Other children used the FM system as their primary source of amplification. Some of the children had received cochlear implants (see Chapter 10). Everyone used the method of receiving sound that worked best for him or her. It depended on the degree and type of hearing loss and the child's level of speech development.

Alec received auditory training and speech therapy twice a week and got to know the other children. The average age was two-and-a-half and there were several small groups, each with a teacher and an assistant. The room was plain, to minimize distractions, acoustically prepared, and had a one-way mirror so parents could watch from the other side of the wall.

One or two concepts were taught at each session. For example, from strands of gift-wrap yarn the children learned colors. Then they learned the word for "hand" and the idea of "down." Sitting on the floor, everyone learned "hands down" from hands in the air to hands on the floor. Finally a handprint was made by each child in turn, following the example of the teacher, with finger paint on construction paper . . . "hands . . . down" . . . with highly satisfactory results and pleased smiles all around. Alec joined in enthusiastically.

At the clinic his parents were also learning how to provide the best language-learning surroundings for Alec at home and how to teach him themselves. They made friends with other parents. This gave them support and lessened their feelings of isolation; other people had similar problems. His parents also had professional counseling.

At home they were imaginative and inventive. How would you go about changing a world that sounds strange and distorted into a place that can be understood, especially for a person still at the beginning of learning what language is all about? Alec's parents used gestures and body language—to show approval and disapproval, for example—adding the words that went with the gestures and making sure every time that he understood. They acted out scenes, drew pictures, clipped photographs and illustrations from magazines. Once the connection was made and the point understood or the word correctly pronounced, a hug did wonders. They not only told him things, they asked him questions and asked for his ideas and opinions, helping him to reason and to use his imagination.

When Alec was old enough to read, his parents added labels to pictures, made scrapbooks of specific topics—a winter day or baking cookies. They used songs and rhymes, word games, and card games. Blank books were filled with photos and words and drawings wherever they went. Cartoons and stories conveyed more difficult abstract ideas. And Alec loved to read.

There were also special workbooks that helped Alec develop his speech according to the normal, natural patterns of learning. His parents tried to make everything fun for him. There was so much to learn, but almost everything had to have a point to it: To increase his vocabulary and ability to communicate in a normal two-way process.

Alec was bright; the problem was to bridge the gap of not hearing, so progress was slow and much patience and time were needed. Alec's parents often got tired and frustrated. Alec got tired and frustrated too. When the reason was a communication difficulty, his parents tried to help him out of it. But sometimes, of course, he acted up or threw tantrums for other reasons, like any other kid. He had to learn the difference between being naughty and its consequences and his outbursts of frustration and the ways they were dealt with differently.

Sometimes they forgot all about learning things and

roughhoused together or went out for ice cream and laughed and had a good time. Hearing loss doesn't mean you have to lose your sense of fun or humor.

Alec went to a regular nursery school to get used to being with hearing—and speaking—children. He enjoyed himself. Young children are more easygoing than older ones when it comes to accepting someone who is a little different. Mostly the children at nursery school took no notice of Alec's hearing aids. When he didn't hear what they were saying, they just told him again until he heard or was helped by the teacher. If anyone asked about the hearing aids, they were explained, and that was that. They saw he was not a hearing-impaired person, but a *person* who happened to have a hearing impairment. Unfortunately this straightforward attitude doesn't always continue as children grow older, or when they become adults.

There are several options for hearing-impaired children once it is time for regular school. About one-third of the children go to private or public residential schools for the deaf either as weekly boarders going home on weekends or, if they live close enough, as day students. Other children go to day schools for the deaf where the program is also organized to meet their special requirements. Children at special residential schools, and certain day schools, usually have profound hearing losses; they mostly use sign language and may or may not speak or have intelligible speech.

Other children go to special classes for hearing-impaired students in local, regular, public schools with specially trained teachers. In New York City, the Board of Education's Hearing Education Services provides a self-contained program at fourteen centers in elementary and junior high schools. "Self-contained" teachers provide all academic and special instruction. Students may play sports and take subjects like art with hearing students. Sometimes they take some subject classes with hearing students, using an interpreter or other help.

Children are often mainstreamed in a regular public

46

school for the whole day or for some classes. Special resources and services should be made available to help: Interpreters, note-takers, assistive listening devices like FM systems, a "buddy" system in the classroom where friends help out. There is a resource room where children are helped individually or in small groups in speech and language and given tutoring in academic subjects where needed. The resource teachers and the classroom teachers work together to help the children as much as possible. The Resource Room Centers program of the New York Board of Education serves twenty-one elementary and intermediate schools in the city. For many students the "self-contained" program leads to this program. New York City's Related Services program operates from a central base, helping students weekly with individual needs.

Most public school teachers have no experience with hearing loss and need help themselves in dealing with hearing-impaired students. The New York Board of Education circulates material to aid teachers explaining lip-reading, for example, and how to help students who use it. Teacher training programs now include a segment on working with hearing-impaired students.

Alec went to a regular public school. Although it would be difficult for him, his parents hoped that with his early start and solid training, public school attendance would eventually help him to fit into the surrounding hearing world.

In elementary school, classes were small and Alec had the same teacher for all of them. He became used to her voice, and whatever adjustments were needed to ensure that he was understanding were made. It was harder for him than for the other children, and he had to have time to rest.

In junior high school it got even harder. This was partly, of course, because schoolwork became more difficult. Subjects like English, with its abstractions and ambiguities, are very complicated to understand if you have not grown up hearing. Think, for example, of the many meanings of words like ''weigh'' and ''way'' (and the spelling too!). Then there are idioms and slang and metaphors like ''she's on her high horse'' or ''building castles in the air.'' Hearing-impaired people are usually better at concrete subjects that have visual components like diagrams.

In high school, classes were larger, teaching was less individual, and different subjects had different teachers. Even with specialized help it was a hard struggle. Alec's parents went over his Individualized Educational Program (IEP) annually with his teachers. The teachers needed to understand that there was nothing wrong with Alec's mind, only with the physical pathways to it. The IEP, stating the kinds of services each child will receive, is mandated by law, but it is sometimes difficult to get it implemented in schools. In New York public schools the High School Centers program offers various kinds of help citywide: Supportive daily instruction by a teacher of the deaf, ''self-contained'' classrooms with subject courses taught by teachers of the deaf, or a combination of both plus support services in areas like assistive devices and guidance services.

Some of the other kids couldn't understand about Alec's hearing problems and teased him when he couldn't hear them or when he sat up in front near the teacher—the best way he could follow what was being said. He knew he was different and would often have felt left out, sad, and lonely if he had not also made some friends. Although the teasers were hurtful, he tried to ignore them. Standing up to them, and even having an occasional fight, cleared the air considerably.

Teasing does not always happen. Many young hearing-impaired people tell of great support among their classmates, some of whom also join sign language courses.

Alec's parents encouraged his independence. It is often easy to overprotect a disabled person. They were worried that his ears, plugged with the hearing aids, might get hurt in sports. They were anxious about letting him go to new places by himself. But they didn't shield him from everyday life. They helped him by practicing "dry runs"; for example, going over a bus ride in advance so he would know the questions he might need to ask and therefore the possible answers.

Technology also helped foster independence. Alec had a telephone device for the deaf (TDD) and was also fortunate that his state had a telephone relay service he could use. (See Chapter 10 for more details on both of these.) While he was in high school he was even luckier. His parents had his home TDD connected to a computer network, considerably broadening his communication possibilities.

During high school he still had weekly speech therapy. And while the others learned Spanish, he had remedial work in English. His parents asked his subject teachers if they would wear an FM microphone and transmitter so that their voices reached him as clearly as possible. Note-taking in class was difficult, however, since he had to keep his eyes on the teacher's face to see what he was saying and could not write at the same time. If Alec got badly stuck he borrowed a friend's notes to copy after class.

He missed a lot of jokes, school talk, and some activities. Often he couldn't keep up with school work and got very tired from the constant need to concentrate on listening. But mostly he felt the positives in his life outweighed the negatives. He became a scout, played sports, and learned to drive. In the summer he earned some money doing paint jobs for neighbors. Very little talking and listening were required, and instructions could be written. His ears needed a rest! He asked girls on dates, and the brown eyes, grin, and curly hair usually were more important than the hearing aids and awkward-sounding speech. He planned to go to college and study computers. He would use the support services of trained note-takers and/or oral interpreters (see

Chapter 7). He tried to do his best for his own satisfaction, without feeling he had to outshine others in order to be accepted as a normal person.

Being an only child made things a bit easier for Alec. His parents could concentrate on his development. In a family with more than one child where one is hearing impaired, the situation is somewhat different. Everyone should get equal attention in a family, but the hearing-impaired child needs more whether he wants it or not. Siblings can be jealous and envious of the extra time given at home and outside the home, like when the deaf child has to be taken for speech therapy. They can be resentful and angry if they don't have their own time with Dad and Mom. Hearing children also have needs, and just because they can hear does not mean they can always get along fine by themselves.

Siblings occasionally feel guilty because they *can* hear and therefore have easier lives. When they are with other people they have to help their sibling understand what is going on, and this slows everything down. They have to help with the language and speech practice. Some may also be secretly afraid of becoming deaf themselves and afraid to share these fears, even though they would be set at rest.

There can be positive aspects in the family situation, too. Good family feelings can develop because one member needs something extra. Siblings are often the chief encouragers and helpers, and a satisfying sense of teamwork and solidarity can be the result.

Hearing-impaired children in the United States whose native language is not English have the added problem of learning a foreign language as well as learning speech itself. Poor or minority parents may not know how and where to get both help for the child's hearing problem and financial aid so they can pay for needed treatment and training. Such problems are not, of course, confined to poor and minority families.

Alec was fortunate in having supportive parents and a supportive environment. He also worked very hard. To have a chance of succeeding orally in the hearing world, a hearing-impaired child needs early discovery of the condition to foster good speech and language development and some residual hearing. He or she needs concentrated teaching from the beginning, appropriate hearing aids and devices, and support services and systems at home and in school—and the will to succeed.

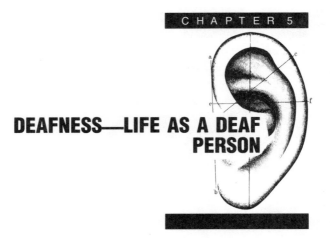

CHAPTER 5

DEAFNESS—LIFE AS A DEAF PERSON

In groups where everyone is deaf, members are part of a shared world and a shared culture. They have always been deaf; they do not know what it is like to hear. Since deafness is an innate characteristic, deaf families do not feel "handicapped" at home or among other deaf people. They often look at their deafness as more of an annoyance than anything else. They realize how much easier and more convenient life would be if they could hear, but deafness is a fact of life that is not going to change, and they have worked out a life-style within that framework.

Everyone in a deaf community communicates in the same way: Manually by sign language—ASL in the United States. The deaf community as an entity, is not, comparatively, a large group; it is comprised of about 500,000 out of two million deaf people in the United States. While people of ethnic or religious minority groups tend to live near one another, members of the deaf community are scattered throughout society. They are a mixture of races, classes, religions, values, intelligence—just like the rest of the people around them. Holding them together is their shared inability to hear, their manual language and avoidance of speech, their education (usually), and their view of the hearing world. Deaf culture is more than a communal lack of hearing; it colors many aspects of life. There is a group identity, a history, and a continuity. Members have a sense of unity, involvement, and mutual support.

Deaf communities have developed since Thomas Hopkins Gallaudet founded the first American school for the deaf, which was a focus for deaf people and for the development of ASL. Deaf history and tradition are transmitted through stories, folktales, and "oral" history—except that the "oral" history is transmitted by the hands.

Personal contact is the most important social aspect of deaf communities. Members meet in a variety of social settings such as schools, clubs, and national networks, and of course at home through personal and family friendships. They also communicate through publications and, more recently, through TDDs. (TDDs, interpreters, and closed caption television are also helping deaf people access what they need in the hearing world without the need to speak themselves.) Sports are very popular; the major organization is the American Athletic Association of the Deaf.

Originally justy social gatherings, the clubs, since the 1960s, have also become centers for political activism. This is also true of local state associations, most of which have joined the National Association of the Deaf (NAD). The NAD, a voluntary, self-help organization, was founded in 1880 in opposition to the Milan Conference's stand on oralism. It is the oldest consumer organization of disabled people in the United States and now has about 20,000 members. It is a major advocate of the deaf to the government and helps deaf people in all areas, from politics and law to jobs, education, and rehabilitation.

Deaf children of deaf parents are often well adjusted because they have the security of a native language and culture from infancy. They have inherited their culture as most of us do and have been in full and natural communication with their families as long as they can remember. For that reason they are often better adjusted than deaf children of hearing parents. A person born deaf in a deaf family is most likely to be a member of the deaf community, growing up signing and knowing other deaf people. But only about nine or ten percent of deaf children have deaf parents. Deaf children with hearing parents, the vast majority, have little or no access to the deaf community. If they do join, it is usually as a young adult or adult. The deaf community is mainly an adult community. Deaf people usually marry other deaf people, but most of the children of these marriages are hearing. So, more often than not, the culture is not inherited but learned, usually at a later age from outside the family.

The focal point of the deaf community has traditionally been the special school for the deaf, particularly the state residential school. The schools have emphasized speech and speechreading because they aimed to integrate their students into the hearing world as much as possible, and most of the teachers have been hearing. Deaf teachers, however, have served as role models and sources of information. Other successful deaf adults and older teenagers have also been role models and helped to transmit the culture. Since signing was traditionally not allowed in most school classes, children got around this by communicating in sign outside classes, in the dorms and playgrounds, teaching one another and educating new students in deaf culture. In the early twentieth century these schools served 90 percent of deaf students, were the center of their lives, and determined the way they would live.

Today, while the schools' goal is to help young deaf people use oral skills, the chief method used in residential schools is Total Communication, with its emphasis on sign. Sign, in fact, is now dominant in residential schools. In earlier times a combined system was used: Oral communication in the elementary grades, and, if this did not continue satisfactorily, Simultaneous Communication (speech and signing together) in the higher grades.

Special schools, whether residential or day, offer very favorable conditions in which deaf children can learn. The environment is geared to lack of hearing. The acoustics are the best possible, using carpeting and acoustic ceiling tiles to absorb sound. Good lighting makes speechreading and signing less strenuous. And, where everyone is deaf, the pressure of competition with those who hear is absent. These conditions are not the "real" world and may to a certain extent isolate children from that reality. (Mainstreaming can also isolate deaf children in regular schools.) Special schools, however, make the learning environment easier.

In residential and day schools for the deaf, classroom teachers have received special training to teach deaf children, and speech therapists give individual training to the students. Counselors help with mental and emotional problems, and audiologists and doctors help with physical hearing needs.

When mainstreaming was introduced, much funding was taken away from the special schools and used in regular school districts for special services. The number of children attending residential schools has declined, a cause for concern to the deaf community. In 1985, the percentage was down to 30 percent. The less severely hearing impaired are partially or fully mainstreamed. Some residential schools have compensated by becoming information and service resource centers for the deaf, for hearing educators, and for the general public. Clarke School in Northampton, Massachusetts, is an example.

Because the majority of deaf people have hearing parents, they do not enter the deaf community at birth. Membership is not automatic; it has to be earned by those truly wanting to join. Occasionally people who are not deaf are accepted: Hearing husbands or wives, friends who may have deaf parents or siblings. Sometimes professionals in the hearing field may become "courtesy" members. All must show a real and honest interest in the fundamental goals of the community, and they must know how to sign. Many friendships exist outside the community between deaf and hearing people.

55

Deaf people have been wary of hearing people's motives throughout history. The hearing world has tried to control the deaf by forcing them to be educated and to operate in an oral system, a system deaf people are not physically equipped to use. Hearing people have forbidden them to use sign language. Many of them "failed" as oral people and then were sent to residential schools, often too late to make up for lost time, even when they used the more flexible combined system. There is still resentment about unfair labels as well as about the need for some dependence on the hearing world. Some members of the deaf community try to have as little contact as possible with it. When they are signing they do so without mouthing words or moving their lips. Speaking, even moving the lips, is a reminder to them of being forced to be oral, to make a "poor imitation of a hearing person out of a deaf one," as deaf historian Jack Gannon puts it.

Many people in the deaf community are more comfortable with the situation and would simply like to be accepted as equals in the world we all share. They are not against speech, just against dogma about communication methods, and their children grow up bilingually, learning sign at home and being taught oral skills at school. With successful education and interaction between the two worlds, deaf people can be comfortable in the hearing world without losing their deaf identity.

Many deaf people are able to speak, but their voices often do not sound natural. They cannot monitor tone and volume and often speak in a monotone or have trouble modulating the sounds appropriately. Since they can't hear their own laughter or crying, it may sound strange to hearing people. It is difficult for them to know what a hiccup or a burp, for instance, sounds like—or even if they make sound at all. Sometimes they may grunt or hum without being aware of it. They may unwittingly be noisy, letting a door bang or scraping a chair, because they cannot know that such things produce unwanted sound.

As we have said, though, they do not live in a silent world. Many hear sounds in the lower frequencies and certainly feel the vibrations that sounds produce. Many deaf people like percussion music and enjoy dancing like anyone else, following the beat and vibrations of the music. A young, deaf Scotswoman, Evelyn Glennie, is a professional percussionist, playing everything from drums to marimba. She "hears" the pitch of the instruments through her body. "I can feel the vibrations," she says, "and I have a kind of mental picture of the sound I'm making."

Society needs to be educated in dealing with the deaf as well as the other way around. Signing often embarrasses hearing people who are unaccustomed to seeing it. They don't understand that facial expressions and body language are part of the language, and they are disturbed. The signers, too, are often embarrassed by the rude stares. Social situations where deaf and hearing people meet can often be stiff and full of misunderstanding. For instance, hearing people often shout at deaf people—as they often misguidedly do to foreigners who don't know their language—thinking that a raised voice will increase intelligibility as well as penetrating the deafness. While a louder tone may well help, shouting is merely rude. It is better to find out what method of communication is easiest for everybody.

Over 90 percent of deaf children are born to hearing parents. They are *a part* of the family but *apart* from it at the same time. The other family members hear: the deaf child does not. No matter how much love and caring abound in the household, the parents cannot know what it feels like to be deaf. The child is to some extent an outsider. Alec, in the last chapter, was in this kind of family situation. Hearing parents usually try to have their deaf children educated in as oral a way as possible to prepare them for a life in the hearing world. Such children live in the world of the hearing and have no access to the deaf community.

57

Hearing parents often do not want their children to sign. They are afraid it will prevent them from learning to speak and that they will only be able to communicate with others who sign. A large proportion of deaf people grow up in the hearing world, live in it as well as they can, and do not learn to sign. Many oral deaf people join the Alexander Graham Bell Association's Oral Deaf Adults section. Some oral deaf people do, however, join the deaf community, feeling their identity belongs more naturally there. People deafened in their teens or later will usually remain in the oral world: Their experiences are those of the hearing world.

The degree of success in learning language and speech, or the decision not to be oral, determines what a deaf person does after completing high school. Residential and special day schools, like regular schools, give vocational and career counseling and help with job placement.

There are several options for postsecondary education. Gallaudet University enrolls more than 2,200 deaf students in its liberal arts programs. (Gallaudet College, by the way, invented the football huddle to enable players to pass strategies secretly to one another.) Signing is very important at Gallaudet, especially since the 1988 election of a deaf president and the affirmation of deaf culture. Many students are bilingual. Classes are held in Simultaneous Communication (Simcom)—spoken and signed at the same time in Signed English or Pidgin Signed English. It is not possible to use English and ASL in Simcom, just as you could not use any other two languages simultaneously. ASL was previously not allowed in the classroom at all except in special circumstances.

Students at Gallaudet University
were outraged when a hearing person
was named as president in 1988.
The students' protests resulted
in the appointment of a deaf president.

58

Graduates go on to professional and management jobs and earn better salaries than other deaf people. Some also become leaders and spokespeople for the deaf community.

Not everyone studies liberal arts, however, and not everyone goes to Gallaudet. There has also been a need for technical education. In 1968, the National Technical Institute of the Deaf (NTID) was founded in Rochester, New York, to provide technical and professional training for approximately 1,000 deaf students in science, technology, and applied arts. As the institute is on the campus of the Rochester Institute of Technology, students can attend classes there as well as or instead of at the NTID.

Regular colleges around the country are now accepting deaf students more readily. Some colleges have separate programs for hearing-impaired students, who are provided with interpreters (oral or sign), tutors, assistive devices, and other support services. In other colleges students are mainstreamed and make arrangements for the support services they need with specialists on the school staff.

Many deaf people go on to successful careers in government, business, and industry. Many also go into careers in the field of deafness. There are, for example, about 1,300 hearing-impaired teachers of the deaf. Others work at technical jobs or at jobs where hearing is less important than visual or manual skills. Traditionally, deaf people worked in areas like carpentry, printing, and the clothing industry, but the deaf have worked at every imaginable job except those that specifically require hearing. Various jobs in the computer industry are popular with deaf people, such as computer programming. Computers also help them to be able to work. Telecommunications, for example, gives access to electronic bulletin boards and networks. Computers are also used as teaching aids.

Many of the deaf, however, are underemployed and often passed over for promotion because of their limited or nonexistent hearing. If they are performing satisfactorily and feel they have been unfairly treated, they can now seek legal recourse.

Many others, because of their profound deafness, the environment they have grown up in, and perhaps their inability to acquire enough basic language skills, have found higher education and success beyond their reach. They have such difficulty with language that they remain several years behind their peers in school. Later they have difficulty being employed. Many jobs, even if not requiring phone use, require speech and language skills. If employed at all, such deaf people are likely to work at unskilled or semiskilled manual jobs. Scientific and technological advances also require higher educational levels than in earlier times.

However, as the labor pool gets smaller because of retirees and slower population growth, the job market may be opening up more for the general disabled population. Affirmative action because of Sections 501 and 504 of Title V of the Rehabilitation Act of 1973 is also helping to get the disabled employed.

Ninety percent seems to be a recurrent figure. We have seen that around ninety percent of deaf children have hearing parents. Ninety is also the percentage of deaf parents with hearing children. These children are also in a non-hereditary situation: They are different from their parents. When they are very young, they take the difference for granted, often not realizing that there is anything out of the ordinary in the family or in their roles as interpreters and links for their parents with the hearing world. They grow up bilingual in English and sign language. Having deaf parents usually does not affect their speech, as they learn it outside the home. Some, in fact, speak particularly clearly, being accustomed to the need for clear speech at home if some speech is used there. Some children are embarrassed by their parents' signing in public. Signing is, however, becoming better known and more familiar. And those who sign are not necessarily deaf. Many hearing people are also learning to sign, out of interest or for career purposes. There are places, too, where signing is clearer than speech—in a noisy subway, for example, where speech is all but impossible.

Attitudes are changing on both sides. Commerce and industry see a new constituency; lawyers and investment bankers now look for deaf clients. Stores and other businesses have TDD numbers, and ads on TV are closed captioned. Technology is helping to bridge the worlds. Cochlear implants may enable more deaf people to hear, and as the technology improves they may be quite comfortable in both worlds. There is a new pride and self-confidence in the deaf community. Dr. Frederick Schreiber, former executive director of the NAD, wrote,

"Ears are cheap. It's what's between them that counts."

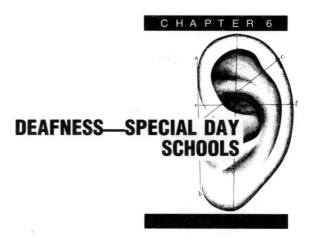

CHAPTER 6

DEAFNESS—SPECIAL DAY SCHOOLS

In the junior high communications class at Lexington School for the Deaf, students are talking about a young adult novel they have just read.

"What happened to the brother?" asks Terri Donaldson, the teacher. She speaks somewhat louder than normal but naturally, holding the FM microphone about six inches from her mouth. Eight pairs of eyes are trained on her face. The students sit at their desks in a semicircle so everyone has a clear view of the teacher and of one another for easier speechreading.

The room is large and bright, the floor carpeted, the ceiling acoustic tiled for sound absorption. Windows fill a wall, but no one is silhouetted against the light: You can't lipread a face in shadow. It is obviously a spot for readers and budding writers. Posters, ideas for journals, writer's tools, and self-editing tips fill the walls. The bookshelves are inviting.

At Lexington, classes are small: six to eight students per class in the lower grades; eight to twelve in high school. One-to-one teaching is necessary when each student has individual hearing needs. The school is a mini United Nations, too. Children come from all over New York State

63

*Students in class at Lexington
pay close attention to the speaker.*

and elsewhere, from various cultures and backgrounds. The unifying force is deafness.

Andrea answers about the brother in the story, the FM system around her neck bouncing as she animatedly describes what's going on in the book. Like everyone else in the class, she is profoundly deaf. Loud noises are the only sounds they can hear without their hearing aids. Andrea wears two aids, both connected to the FM system for the class. Some kids at the school wear only one aid if the second ear cannot be helped by amplification. A few wear none, either because they rely on speechreading, or because they are new and have not yet started using them. A few simply refuse to wear them.

Andrea's voice sounds pretty normal. She has been a student at Lexington since she was a baby. Her first hearing aids were fitted in the Infant Center, and she has had speech, language, and auditory training ever since—it's an integral part of her education. She is an excellent candidate for mainstreaming if she wants to transfer for high school. Lexington helps such students get the needed services and support in regular schools. A successful transfer depends on the individual school, the student, and even the student's age. What works at one age doesn't necessarily work at another. Transfers happen in the other direction when a student comes to Lexington from a public school. These kids often find the academic program at the public school they've left more demanding and the standards higher than they are at Lexington. But at Lexington they are not left out of anything, they are not different, and they are among peers. At Lexington everyone has a better chance to shine, to be class president, or just to be themselves.

Lexington School for the Deaf sits squarely and solidly in the middle of a section of small rowhouses and gardens in Jackson Heights, New York. It dominates the surrounding area, testimony to its position as the fourth largest school for the deaf in the United States. It is part of the Lexington Center, which comprises the Department of Special Services (including Interpreter Services and Advocacy, among others), the Research and Training Division (for example, a recreational and vocational program for young adults), Mental Health Services, and the Hearing and Speech Center (including, for example, audiological services and speech-language pathology).

Lexington School is a special day school for deaf infants, children, and teens—altogether over 400 students. The school is registered by the New York State Department of Education and is free to residents of New York

State. Founded in 1867, it has long been a leader in deaf education.

In many ways Lexington is a regular school with a regular curriculum. There's a pool, a gymnasium, and athletic fields, as well as a library-media center and an auditorium. All regular subjects are taught: Science, math, English, social sciences. Nonacademic subjects include dance and art.

As long as a subject has visual components, it is easier to learn. In math, for instance, there is an emphasis on computation, which can be described on a blackboard. Much other academic learning is verbal and abstract, though. It's harder to show and explain visually and therefore harder to understand. Computers are increasingly being used as classroom aids.

Right from the start, special emphasis is put on speech and language development and auditory training. The Infants Program, for babies through three years of age, gets children off to an early head start, essential for a child missing normal and constant exposure to language and the resulting effortless learning. Starting late may make deaf children fall more and more behind, setting them back perhaps for years.

At kindergarten and elementary school levels, teaching is chiefly oral, although the system has been changing to accommodate some sign. Sign is in greater use in high school.

Teachers and support staff are specially trained to work with deaf children. The pace and rhythm are easy and relaxed; the teacher makes sure everyone understands and interprets where necessary. The ultimate goal is, of course, to help students achieve a high enough level of speech and language, including reading and writing, to have an easier life in the world in which they will live.

Since it is extremely difficult to learn to speak if you have little or no input of sound and cannot hear your own voice, children learn by using their eyes and sense of touch along with whatever aided residual hearing they have. That is, auditory training is coupled with visual and often tactile training.

Some aspects of speech can be seen, and children learn by watching lip, tongue, and jaw movements very carefully. You can also feel sound. Sound makes vibrations in various areas of the head, face, throat, and chest. You can feel your own muscle movements as you speak. Put your fingers on your throat and say the last three sentences aloud. Can you feel the motions? Different sounds vibrate in different areas. Maybe you also noticed your breath helping you produce the sounds. A deaf child learns this way, touching the teacher's throat or nose, for example, and trying to imitate the vibrations, learning to reproduce the sound correctly. It is a very difficult way to learn speech, and it can take weeks to perfect a single sound.

Vibro-tactile devices are now being developed to help in this method of learning speech. Some devices provide fairly simple tactile clues. Vibrators or electrodes touching the skin make the person aware of sound patterns and intensity through a microcomputer-based "voice analyzer." Skin is very sensitive. One vibrator device, held in the hand or applied to the wrist, feels like an intermittently buzzing insect. Another, more complicated, stimulates the skin with electrical impulses that feel like a tapping finger.

Experiments with vibro-tactile training are currently being conducted at Lexington School, a leader in the field. Sensors are placed inside the mouth and on the nose of both the speech therapist and the child and connected to a computer. Sounds or words produced by the therapist are shown as a pattern on the computer screen. The child feels the electrodes, which help him move his tongue, lips, and jaw in the right ways in order to pronounce the sound. At the same time he tries to match the pattern on the screen and so reproduce the sound correctly. The screen can also show the position of the therapist's tongue for making different sounds, and the student can copy what he sees. Other charts show the vibrations in the therapist's nose as she speaks and the loudness of her voice.

Part of the schedule at Lexington are remedial speech sessions using the IBM Speech Viewer. Wayne is in fifth grade. His mother and sister were both graduates of Lexington. He sits in front of the computer screen. As Mrs. Hollander, his teacher, speaks into the microphone, "fa . . . fa . . . fa," then "fish . . . fish . . . fish," her voice is shown as a steady, progressive, horizontal pattern. She passes the mike to Wayne, who tries to copy the pattern she has made. He lingers too long on the "-sh" sound. They work at shortening it. The feedback on the screen shows him what he is saying. Wayne builds and practices his speech skills by playing video "games" and responding to pictures and cartoon-style characters and scenes. The Speech Viewer has twelve modules teaching different aspects of speech production. Today Wayne is working on pitch control and on the timing of voicing—that is, how long to continue producing a sound.

Speech therapy might be boring and exhausting in a face-to-face drill across a table with straight repetition and constant struggling. With tools like Speech Viewer the struggle is still there, but it is definitely more fun.

In Mrs. Donaldson's communications class, Peter is explaining what has happened to the hero of a story. Leaning forward to emphasize his point, he notices he is blocking someone's view. He leans back—everyone has to be able to see everyone else's face. While there is a lot of interaction in the class and everyone is eager to give an opinion, only one person talks at a time. Hearing-impaired people cannot follow one conversation if another is going on simultaneously.

Like Andrea, Peter is very verbal, though he is a slower, more effortful speaker. Some of the students have less intelligible speech. For a deaf person, speaking clearly has nothing to do with intelligence. It may depend on the quality of the residual hearing. Some people are able to achieve clear speech better than others. Peter, like the others in his class, signs as he speaks, using the manually coded system of sign he has learned informally. For most of its history Lexington has been an oral school. In the last ten years or so Total Communication has been introduced, chiefly in the higher grades. Sign is learned and used, but not formally taught. A teacher will give a sign if it is needed in the natural course of speaking. Otherwise, in class the teacher speaks—with or without an FM system—and uses gestures and other aids to speechreading. The students most often pick up sign from one another.

As they grow up, students become more aware of their identity as deaf people; signing is central to this self-awareness and becomes part of their mode of communication. When they graduate they have the option to choose which modes of communication they prefer to use and which they are most successful in.

Younger children are more oral; in the middle grades many use Simcom. The older students use more sign—often to the detriment of their speech skills. Many children at Lexington come from deaf families who sign; many are from the deaf community. It is easy and natural for signing to become a part of communication.

If oral education is not successful, children are able to transfer to a school with a signing program. Lexington naturally likes to succeed with its students, hence the introduction of some signing into its program.

Social life is, of course, very important, especially since many of the students go home to hearing families and communities. School friends can visit, and, if a student's family can't afford a telephone device for the deaf (TDD), the school will lend one, with the parents' permission. Like Alec earlier in this book, Lexington students join the Scouts or Little League and take part in many of the extracurricular activities most kids enjoy.

There are no bells for the end of class—no one would hear them. Mrs. Donaldson announces the homework as-

69

signment and gets up. Burt touches Peter to get his attention. They plan to meet for basketball practice over the weekend. There's a general ducking for backpacks and a surge to the door, to the school bus, to the weekend.

Which system of education is best for hearing-impaired children? It depends on the individual child's abilities, personality, and background. Teachers and other professionals in the hearing field, parents, and support groups create a suitable environment to help the child achieve the best possible results.

How about modes of communication? Should a child sign or speak? Sign first or speak first? Learn to speak or read first? Sign *and* speak? There is still much controversy and discussion and as yet no "best" answer.

Some experts say that since the deaf child's best means of communication is visual, sign should be first. The child can then learn about his environment and develop fluency and confidence in a way that parallels the development of hearing children. Once there is a successful input method, improving the use of residual hearing and learning to speak can follow and will be easier. Or a child can continue to build visual communication skills.

Those who favor the oral method say that we live in a hearing world, and those who cannot cope with it will be isolated and have lower expectations and possibilities in life. Since signing is easier, educators worry that children will not want to develop the more difficult speaking skills after learning sign. Auditory/oral training must be begun early and continued intensively. Once language based on auditory input is established, sign can be learned.

Whichever mode is learned first, aiming for bilingualism would appear to be a sensible goal. And the ultimate decision of which method of communication to use is finally up to the deaf person.

Deafness in itself is not the problem; the problem is *communication,* and through it access to a full life.

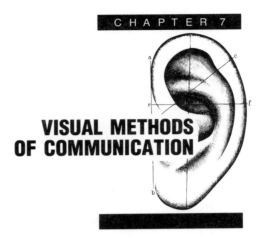

VISUAL METHODS
OF COMMUNICATION

You may have thought there was just one sign language and one way of communicating visually: Using your hands. At its most basic level this would seem to be true. But you have already seen that no one uses a single means of communication. When you speak you also use gestures and facial expressions that go with what you are saying. A totally blank face or the wrong expression for the context confuses or misleads the hearer; if you say, "I am happy" with a frown on your face, it's hard to know what you really mean. Similarly the tone or emphasis in your voice gives a clue to meaning. *"I* am happy" presupposes "but *you* are not." "I *am* happy" with your fists clenched may be said in defiance of the facts. You might, incidentally, also be speaking in English or Spanish or Japanese. . . .

Without hearing, normal acquisition of speech and language is closed off. But sign language can be accessible and attainable.

Sign languages are full and complete languages, like English, Spanish, or Japanese. And there are British sign language, Spanish sign language, and Japanese sign language, as well as a host of others, including American Sign Language (ASL). Each of these languages has its own grammar, vocabulary, and idioms. They are able to convey abstract as well as concrete ideas. The difference is that sign languages are not spoken; they are created to be *seen*. Sign language is a formal visual/gestural system so people can communicate without the spoken or written word. Signs and accompanying body language are the words, expression, and emphasis of the language.

Meaning is conveyed by handshapes and their movements and positions in relation to the face, body, and each other. Signing is three-dimensional, using the immediate space surrounding the person together with facial expressions and body language. Several dialects of ASL are used throughout the United States and Canada. No formal written version yet exists, so children having ASL as their native language have to learn to read and write in English. Sign language is accepted by nearly thirty universities in the United States as a foreign language option.

Why not a universal sign language? One has been attempted—Gestuno—the way Esperanto has been attempted as a universal spoken language, but neither has had much success. ASL and other sign languages have developed over time according to different patterns of different countries and cultures. But while there are no universal sign languages, certain aspects of grammar (though not of meaning) seem to be held in common.

You know some signs already. If someone signed ''I am angry'' or ''I have a book,'' you would understand

I   angry

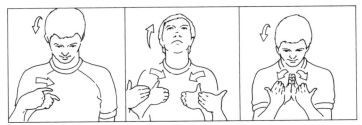

'I have a book.'

immediately. But as ASL is not a mimed version of speech, most of it has to be learned like any foreign language. Grammar must be learned. For example, changes in movement, direction, and space show changes in the meanings of verbs and pronouns, as in

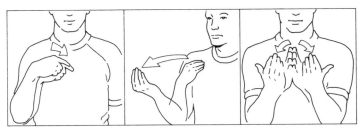

'I give her the book.'

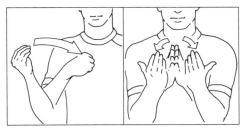

'She gives me the book'

73

Time (past, present, and future tense) is expressed by adding to a sign rather than adding extra words as in English. In the sentence
"That's far into the future,"
the length of time is rendered by the sign for "future"

Far into the future

repeated farther away. In conversation, the time frame is established at the beginning and is only indicated again if it changes. Repetition gives extra power to meaning. An adjective like "beautiful," for example, signed with emphasis and repeated becomes "very beautiful." Facial expressions and body language are also part of grammar. Raising eyebrows and frowning slightly, for example, signals a question. Try it yourself; it's very clear.

The basics of ASL can be learned in a few months, but it takes time and practice to be fluent. And, like any language, it is constantly evolving and changing. ASL, signed by a person sensitive to language, is beautiful and expressive just as bad signing is ugly and inelegant. ASL is the nonspoken native language of many deaf people.

The *manual alphabet*—fingerspelling—is a very useful partner to ASL. The twenty-six letters of the alphabet are formed by the fingers "spelling" in the air, and are used for proper names and words with no ASL equivalent. It's also a way for a hearing person to cue a deaf person in to an oral conversation. The manual alphabet can be learned

American Manual Alphabet

(Signs shown as they appear to the person reading them.)

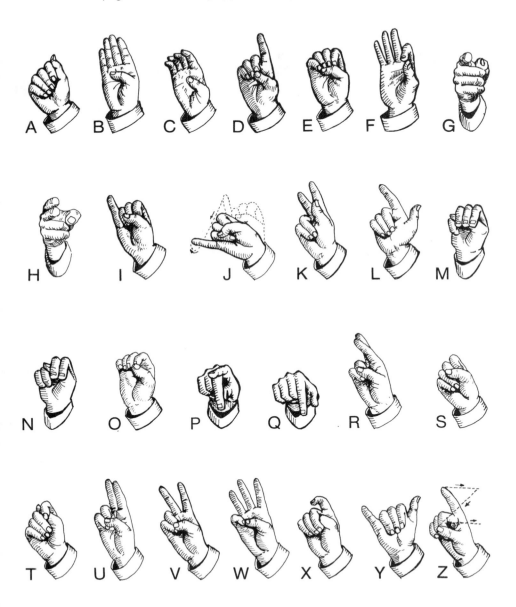

quickly. It is useful if you know a deaf person, and is a slow but perfectly clear method of communication if you don't sign and the other person does not speak. It can also be used as a private code between you and a friend. The British manual alphabet uses two hands—an even better code since few people know it in the United States.

In schools for the deaf, different systems of communication are used. The *Combined Method* just means that both a manual and an oral method are used in a school. For instance, an oral system in the earliest grades (or even in infancy), is combined with a manual communication system in the higher grades.

There are other combinations of communication methods. *Simultaneous Communication* (Simcom), as you have seen, is the use of speech, (spoken aloud or mouthed), signing, and fingerspelling at the same time. It is often used between hearing and deaf people, and it is the system most frequently used in schools for the deaf in the United States. It is also used at Gallaudet University and the NTID. The benefit of the system is that the deaf person, helped where possible by hearing aids and assistive devices, has two ways of understanding what is being said.

Problems come up, though, because of the differences between speaking and language and between the spoken and written word. ASL and English are two different languages. It is not possible to use ASL with English for Simcom because of the differences in grammar and word order. Simcom attempts to convey the same meaning verbally and manually at the same time in order to present language in a visually clear way. Instead of ASL, the signs used in Simcom are from one or another of several *manually coded systems* for English. These systems are intentionally constructed with rules and invented and altered signs, in addition to signs from ASL. They were created in the 1970s for use in schools and in homes with hearing parents and deaf children. These systems try to put the English language into signing form and are used with spoken English so a deaf child can understand and learn to speak more easily. The signs are arranged in the same word order as the spoken language. It is a way to bridge the gap between speaking and signing.

The best known of these systems are *Signed English, Seeing Essential English* (SEE 1), and *Signing Exact English* (SEE 2). The creators of SEE 1 and SEE 2 developed specific signs for articles (like *the*), various parts of speech (conjunctions, prepositions, pronouns), auxiliaries (like *is, are*), and verb inflections (*-s, -ed, -ing,* for example). These signs are used when there is no sign in ASL or a sign exists but has several different English meanings. An ASL user would leave them out, fingerspell them, or show them in some other way. The differences between SEE 1 and SEE 2 are due more to philosophy and approach than to basic differences in construction.

Signed English is also a tool for learning English. It is simpler in structure than the others and corresponds to English word for word. Each sign corresponds to a word in a standard dictionary—not the spelling, letters, or sound of the word, but the word itself. Signed English is somewhat slow to use. There are some 3,100 sign words in Signed English—those most often used—and many of the signs are from ASL. In addition to the sign words there are fourteen sign markers. When one of these is added to the sign word it adds to the meaning, changing present to past, for example, or singular to plural. As the vocabulary is fairly limited, fingerspelling is also used.

When these systems are properly and consistently used, reading and language skills of deaf students can be improved.

Pidgin Sign English (PSE) is not an invented system. It is a mixture of English and ASL using English word order and a largely ASL vocabulary. It enables people who do not sign well and deaf people who know little English to communicate. ''Pidgin'' just means simplified speech used for contact where there is no mutual language. It is

77

an attempt to meet the other person halfway and is neither one language nor the other.

All these systems may seem to complicate the effort to relate the two languages. Someone has called them a Tower of Babel of systems, but the point they make is that in order to learn English, a deaf child must see it. They are not meant to replace ASL, but many deaf people are afraid that these systems are becoming part of the language, changing it and spoiling it.

Simcom is one type of *Total Communication*, which, as you saw in Chapter 3, is a system that uses any and all methods of communication: Signing, speech, gestures, speechreading, fingerspelling, hearing aids, the written word, auditory training—whatever results in the most successful understanding and whatever works best for a specific person in a particular situation. Of course not all of these modes of communication are used at once! The good thing about Total Communication is that it does not force a person into a single, possibly uncongenial, mode of communication. It allows for freedom of choice and individual needs.

Not all visual methods include sign. *Lipreading,* also called *speechreading,* is a visual aid to communication used to understand the spoken language better. It is something everyone does to a certain extent, hearing or hearing impaired, consciously or not, because it is an aid to hearing in general. Its main requirement is careful observation of visual clues. It can be helpful to the hearing impaired because one can see some of the speech sounds and even words, particularly if the context is known. Gestures, facial expressions, and body language (hence the broadening of the term from lipreading to speechreading) add more clues to understanding. Good speechreading is a skill, and one that can be learned, but even the best speechreaders cannot see a whole conversation. Only about 30 percent of English sounds are visible on the lips. And of that 30 percent, half are confusing because while they look alike, their meanings are quite different, for example, bat, mat, pat. Consonants are higher pitched and therefore harder to hear, particularly *s, t, f, p* and the diphthongs *sh* and *ch*. Unfortunately consonants are more important for understanding than vowels. You can't understand this sentence using only its vowels:

..O.   ..EA.   ..EE..   I.   .E..

But you probably can, using only the consonants:

SL.W   CL..R   SP..CH   .S   B.ST

Let's do some speechreading so that you can see for yourself. Sit in front of a mirror so you can watch your face. Say silently, without using your voice:

I MADE THE BED.

See how the same lip movements are used for

I BAKED THE BREAD.

Or try to differentiate visually between "fine" and "vine" or "ship" and "chip." "I offered her coffee" is a different problem because "offer" and "coffee" look identical. "Her cat ate her old canary" is invisible on the lips. Groups of sounds that look alike on the lips are called *homophones:* m, p, b; f, v; sh, ch; w and r are almost alike. Many speech sounds are hidden inside the mouth and throat, like k, g, s, h.

So why bother with speechreading at all? It is a lot of work—and guesswork—even using amplified, residual hearing. And constant practice is needed to improve skills. Some people become very good at it. Knowing the context of the conversation and anticipating what is likely to be said helps considerably with speechreading. You must look at a person's face and read his or her body language. You use your general knowledge, your common sense, filling in the gaps, guessing the most likely word or phrase in the circumstances. You don't need every word, only the gist of the meaning.

Hearing-impaired people may appear slow because they need time to process sound and discriminate among the component parts of language. But their minds and imaginations work like lightning! They are trying to figure out in a microsecond which of all the possibilities is the right one, and at the same time listen and watch to catch the following parts of the conversation, perhaps among a group of people in less-than-ideal listening circumstances. Speechreading is a strain even if you have had training, but if you are hearing impaired you must do it all the time.

Cued Speech was invented in the 1960s as a manual reinforcement system to help people speechread more easily. It consists of eight hand shapes held in four different positions near the face. Each shape and position is a cue to which letters are meant out of those that look the same. The hand *shapes* identify different consonants; the *positions* help to identify vowels. When these cues are used with speech, the hearing-impaired watcher gets the same information that a hearing person gets through the ears. Cued speech can be learned in a few days, even in a few hours, but it takes some months of practice to use it really well. Its chief drawback is that few people know about it.

Interpretation is a different kind of communication aid, and a new and growing profession. It gives the deaf access to the hearing world without needing to hear and speak. Interpreting translates information from one language into another. Between deaf and hearing people it also concerns the shift from an aural to a visual mode. Interpreters can be sign language interpreters or oral interpreters; some people can do both. An interpreter can be deaf or hearing. They are trained professionals. The national *Registry of Inter-*

80

preters of the Deaf (RID), their professional organization, was founded in 1964 and now has over 3,000 members. The RID offers a certificate of proficiency for members and nonmembers—required in several states—establishing standards of competence. Interpreters uphold the RID's code of ethics: "Confidentiality, impartiality, and integrity."

A *sign language interpreter* listens to the hearing speaker and gives exact information to the deaf recipient in sign language. If a deaf person cannot or chooses not to speak, the interpreter will translate that person's signing into speech for the hearing recipient. Sign language interpreters act as a person's ears and voice. Interpreting can be easy, for a simple conversation, or extraordinarily difficult, as in a legal case on a technical subject.

An *oral interpreter* acts as a support system for the hearing-impaired speechreader who does not sign. The interpreter repeats the speaker's words *without sound.* Oral interpreting offers the best possible conditions for the use of speechreading skills and uses natural, clear, unexaggerated lip movements and gestures. It takes practice to follow an oral interpreter, but once the skill is acquired the speechreader can concentrate on the context and worries less about the mechanics of following speech.

The interpreter and client decide in advance whether a word-for-word repetition is wanted or if some rewording is preferred for conciseness. Content and meaning are never changed. So if the speaker is producing garbage, the interpreter interprets garbage!

Under Section 504 of the Rehabilitation Act of 1973, most state agencies will provide interpreters, if needed, for hearing-impaired students. Hearing-impaired people have a legal right to an interpreter in certain situations receiving public funding, such as a criminal or civil court action initiated by the government or in certain hospital emergency situations.

Interpreting is tiring; at a lecture or other lengthy meeting usually two interpreters work together so that one

81

can rest and regain energy after twenty or thirty minutes of work.

Almost all hearing-impaired people use one or more of the communication methods we have looked at.

By the way, these ASL signs may come in handy:

Sign, sign language

Hello, hi

I love you

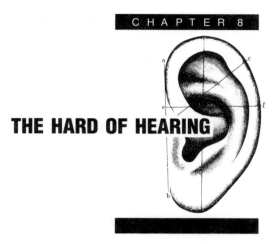

CHAPTER 8

THE HARD OF HEARING

Most of our discussion so far has been about the deaf. What is the dividing line between "deaf" and "hard of hearing"? You learned the basic definitions in Chapter 2, but in reality there is no hard and fast rule to say where "hard of hearing" ends and "deaf" begins.

The hard-of-hearing population occupies a kind of in-between world; they are neither deaf nor normal hearing so they don't fit into either of those worlds, although like being deaf and like being hearing it is just as invisible a condition. At one end of the scale, those who have a severe to profound hearing loss identify in many ways with the deaf, although they will be unlikely to join the deaf community. At the other end are those with a mild loss who can be helped by hearing aids and lipreading to live an almost normal life. But the vast majority of people with hearing loss—between sixteen and eighteen million—occupy a gray area in the middle.

A hearing loss may be inherited, acquired during birth, or develop later through illness, trauma, aging, or other reasons. The hard of hearing start out in life with basic hearing—the majority are, in fact, normal hearing—and so they can develop speech and language. This is the main

83

difference between them and the deaf: They are oral. They have enough residual hearing, with or without hearing aids, and knowledge of the hearing world to communicate verbally. Some may learn sign language; an increasing number use a variety of communication aids; whether consciously or not, all use lipreading. The problem is how and by how much the disability affects the way they can function.

Most hearing losses are gradual and progressive, so the person may end up as deaf as anyone in the deaf community, but with a totally different outlook. Although the end result, difficulties with communication, may be identical, the hard of hearing are different from the deaf. As a deaf person said to a hard-of-hearing person, "You lost something, I didn't," and the other replied, "I had something, you didn't."

There are different types of hearing loss. The most common type is *sensorineural* loss, when there is damage to the inner ear system. It is usually progressive and at present is irreversible. This is the hardest kind of loss to treat and live with. A *conductive* loss, usually resulting from outer and/or middle ear obstruction, may be reversible and can be helped by hearing aids. A *mixed* loss has both sensorineural and conductive elements. A *central* hearing impairment which is rare—happens when there is damage to the auditory route to the brain. As you saw in Chapter 2, a hearing loss may be mild, moderate, severe, or profound and may progress along the scale.

Although hearing loss among young people is increasing, about 75 percent of hard-of-hearing people start losing their hearing in adulthood. Hearing loss in the elderly may be caused by degeneration through the natural process of aging and is called *presbycusis,* from Greek, meaning "old age hearing." About one in four elderly people in the United States have a significant hearing loss, and about half of those over sixty-five have enough loss to make communication uncomfortable. Elderly people are often afraid of admitting their hearing loss in case people think they are becoming senile. The two conditions do not necessarily have any connection.

Diseases connected with hearing loss include *otosclerosis,* a progressive, often hereditary disorder that occurs when the stapes become fixed to the bony part of the inner ear and can no longer vibrate, leading to a conductive hearing loss. If untreated, a further, mixed loss can result. The condition can often be corrected. In the 1930s, surgery called *fenestration* restored useful levels of hearing. Since the 1950s a new technique of surgery called a *stapedectomy* is the preferred procedure. The stapes is removed and a wire inserted to replace it—a simple idea, but one of the most delicate and difficult of all operations.

Ménière's syndrome is a disorder of the inner ear, often affecting only one ear. People have severe vertigo (dizziness) often accompanied by vomiting, a feeling of fullness or pressure in the ear, and *tinnitus,* ringing in the ears. Attacks can last a few minutes to several hours and they can be frequent or absent for years at a time.

Tinnitus is not a disease and can be experienced by itself, usually by older people. Normally our ears are quiet unless outside sound stimulates them. However, slight abnormalities in the cochlea can produce sounds inside the ear. The noises can seem like roars, whines, whistles, or other sounds and can be constant or can come and go. It can be annoying and, if particularly intrusive, can seriously disrupt a person's life. The causes can be noise, wax against the eardrum, infection, substance abuse, allergies, and elevated blood pressure, among others. There is at present no cure, but the person can get some relief. Playing soft music on a radio can cover the noise. Maskers, small, battery-operated devices that fit in the ear, produce "white noise" that can mask the tinnitus and have a soothing, calming effect. Relaxation techniques and stress reduction can also help. People with normal hearing may have tinnitus; deaf people may not have it at all.

85

Sensorineural hearing loss, like being hard of hearing altogether, is not something that can be easily defined. People describe it as being underwater, in a fog, or having a glass wall between them and the speaker. The reason for these descriptions—and the chief problem—is that sensorineural loss can distort and warp speech. One can hear the *sounds* of people talking but have trouble discriminating the *words*. Hearing aids can make the voices louder but not clearer. Background noise, filtered out by normal ears, is merely amplified by hearing aids together with the speaking voices so that a hard-of-hearing person at, say, a party, has the sound of Niagara Falls thundering in his or her ears while trying to pick out and decipher individual voices and understand what they are saying. Communication is easiest one-on-one with no competing background sounds.

Many hard-of-hearing people have a random ability to hear; someone likened it to "Swiss cheese hearing." There are gaps in their hearing processes. Sometimes they can hear a whole sentence if it is at the right pitch and entirely miss the next one. Distortion of sound means that many hard-of-hearing people cannot listen to music because what was once Mozart or musicals or country is now cacophony. The range of hearing is also limited: Sensorineural loss usually cuts out the higher frequencies so that women's and children's voices and high-pitched sounds are eliminated. Deep sounds and voices are easier to hear and understand.

A further annoyance is *recruitment*. The ears, though deaf to many sounds, can be agonizingly sensitive to noise. This is because sound reception has been condensed into a narrow range. When both ears are impaired, localizing sound is another problem; a person can't tell where a sound is coming from.

All this adds up to a very stressful living situation. Hard-of-hearing people have to concentrate all the time on what normally hearing people do without any effort at all.

People struggling to listen all day long under such circumstances become tired, irritable, and stressed. Too much listening under difficult conditions can even make a person ill. Rest and relaxation are necessary periodically. It's not surprising that hard-of-hearing people actually hear better when they are fresh and rested.

Hearing loss can be sudden and dramatic—and thus traumatic. The causes may be physical, mental, or emotional. Occasionally it is psychosomatic; a person shuts off painful experiences by shutting off his or her ears and simply refusing to take in any more on the subject.

But for most people hearing loss creeps up gradually, almost imperceptibly. The first signs may be difficulty on the phone, the feeling that people are mumbling, the need to turn up the TV or radio or to have people repeat what they say. One just doesn't get the words the way one used to.

Some people who realize what is happening go straight to the "hearing health care team." Their regular doctor may send them to an otolaryngologist (an ear, nose and throat specialist) or an otologist (a medical ear specialist) or straight to an audiologist (a hearing specialist), who tests their hearing and tells them whether a hearing aid will help or not. If so, the person is fitted with an aid or aids and counseled on how to use them and live with them as successfully as possible. Assistive listening devices are described to them and perhaps some are acquired. The person learns to cope in the new situation and while not "cured," finds life easier than before.

But for the majority of people who learn they are beginning to lose their hearing, the realization is by no means so simple and the rehabilitation, if achieved, neither so smooth nor so successful. There is a psychological effect to losing one's hearing that parallels losing a loved one. A period of mourning and adjustment is needed. After all, one is losing something precious: the proper working of a vital sense.

87

Such a person is Nora. Her first reaction is denial, a refusal to accept the facts: "This isn't happening to me." People are naturally afraid of losing life as they know it. They see they are beginning to be cut off, and they try to deny it. Often Nora blames her hearing loss on outside situations and people: "You know I can't hear you when the water's running . . ."

Perhaps the hardest stage comes when Nora understands that the problem is permanent. She becomes very angry and rages at everyone, including herself. "Why me? What have I done to deserve this?"

A period of sadness and depression follows as Nora begins to realize how the hearing loss will affect her life. Noticing that many former avenues of communication are becoming increasingly difficult or impossible to use, Nora starts to withdraw. She has difficulty coping with many situations. She is becoming isolated from the sound of almost everything that matters to her—people, music, birds, rain, as well as the more practical sounds that localize and warn. Yet she welcomes the isolation in a way; it is easier to be by oneself with no stresses, strains, or challenges. She is exhausted by efforts to cope and afraid of the future. Becoming dependent on others for many things adds to the feeling of insecurity.

Gradually Nora accepts the situation. She doesn't like it, but it's there for good and she realizes there's nothing wrong with *her,* only with her hearing. Once she has accepted this, she can start adjusting and coping. She will begin to redefine herself and her life-style. There will still be anger and depression, but she will cope with them. She gradually learns a whole new communication strategy based on the simple plan to find and use whatever works for her.

There are many ways of coping. First, of course, is to get hearing aids if they will help and some of the listening devices that make life more secure and reopen some closed doors. We will be talking about these in the next chapter. Here we will just say that knowing when the doorbell is ringing, being able to use the phone again, or watching captioned TV can give a person a feeling of being in control of his or her life once more.

Nora also takes a course in assertiveness training. People who can't hear properly often lose their self-esteem. They need to be spoken to slowly and clearly so that words don't meld into a blur, making them feel "stupid" because of their apparent slowness and their difficulty in understanding. Social skills are undermined when a person often loses the thread or does not keep up. Just missing an added "no" or "not" can radically change the meaning of a sentence. Some people become timid and passive. Some people go the other way, becoming aggressive and demanding their rights in a way that offends.

Hearing people can consciously or unconsciously add to the hard-of-hearing person's insecurity by excluding them from the conversation or ignoring them. Impatience, annoyance, and ridicule are other confidence shakers. Assertiveness training teaches Nora how to stand up for her needs and rights in a positive way, neither passively nor aggressively.

Nora also takes a speechreading course. She learns that she can understand a surprising amount of conversation through speechreading, visual clues, context, and common sense. Although listening isn't always successful for her, it's much better than before.

Nora could possibly benefit from audiotherapy. Attending one-hour sessions twice a week for three to five months, she would learn to make the best use of her residual hearing. Earphones connected to a special machine act as a master hearing aid. The area in which Nora perceives speech most clearly would be found and used. The client repeats what the therapist says without visual clues—the therapist's face is hidden by a book or sheet of paper. Gradually Nora would learn to listen better, using her hearing aids and visual clues in quiet and then also in noisy situations.

Counseling may also help Nora manage stress and help her family cope with her loss, as well. Alternative therapies and treatments like biofeedback and relaxation techniques are also available. Some people try acupuncture and hypnosis. When the inner ear is damaged, physical improvement in hearing can't be hoped for. Science does not yet know how to regrow damaged cochlear hair cells. But any treatment that makes for a more relaxed person and attitude makes listening less of a strain.

Apart from formalized programs and alternative therapies, there are some strategies that are useful for the hearing-impaired person trying to manage in various situations and for the hearing people communicating with them: Family, friends, business people, or even strangers. It is remarkable how the hard of hearing are magnets for people asking directions in any noisy public place!

This list shows how to communicate with a hard-of-hearing person for the best results on both sides:

1. Get the person's attention before speaking.
   Touch lightly—no need to knock out or half-strangle.
2. Face the person so he/she can speechread you.
3. No need to shout.
   Speak normally and clearly, and not too fast. Visual clues and gestures can help.
4. Stand so that your face is in the light.
   If you are silhouetted against the light your face can't be seen for speechreading.
5. Don't talk with your mouth full!
   Chewing makes speech unclear and less visible.
6. Rephrase unheard or misunderstood words in a new way rather than just repeating.
7. Choose a quiet spot away from background noise.
8. Ask what you can do to make conversation easier.
9. Be patient! He/she is trying hard to understand.
10. Relax! He/she is a person just like you.

Of course there are two sides to communication and the hard-of-hearing person has to have some courtesy and common sense, too. Nora should organize her immediate environment in the best way possible. She should tell people she is hard of hearing, explain her needs, and then concentrate on what is being said. Instead of saying "What?" when she doesn't hear, she should say something like, "I got what you said until . . ." She should have a pad and pencil for names, context words, or change of subject keywords. And there's no harm in her thanking someone for their efforts to ensure that she is part of the conversation.

Laws are making life easier, mandating the use of assistive listening devices in certain public places like airports, federal buildings, and public meeting places. The Technology-Related Assistance Act of 1988 helps individual states develop programs of assistance for all ages and disabilities. For hard-of-hearing people this means access to listening devices in a variety of settings.

In the workplace, laws such as the Americans with Disabilities Act of 1990 prevent discrimination against disabled people. If a person can do the job when the appropriate conditions are met, he or she should be hired. A hearing-impaired person is no different from anyone else. At school, Public Law 94–142 mandates that mainstreamed hard-of-hearing children have the assistance and services they require.

Hearing-impaired people can go to concerts and the theater and hear by using infrared systems. Some hospital programs train staff and use special stickers so that the staff are aware of hearing-impaired patients' needs, making hospital stays less traumatic. The travel and hotel businesses are realizing that hard-of-hearing people have money to spend and are making their environments more accessible. This is also true in some investment banking houses.

Support groups can be a continuing morale booster, a

way of making new friends and of learning what's new in the field. Group involvement makes people realize they are not alone: There are other people with the same problem who know what it feels like. In the United States, for example, there is Self Help for Hard of Hearing People, Inc. (SHHH). In Britain there is the British Association for the Hard of Hearing, and worldwide there is the International Federation of the Hard of Hearing.

Even with satisfactory adjustment and help, hard-of-hearing people can sometimes be difficult to deal with because of the trouble they are having. They can be short tempered and irritable. They often monopolize conversations because while they are speaking at least they know what is being said! They can forget that other people may have problems and disabilities too; no one goes through life without any troubles at all. Sometimes they forget that it is not necessary to hear everything or be a part of everything.

It is important not to take oneself too seriously, Nora learns. She is aware of the senses she still has and of all the things she *can* do. She knows she must keep her sense of humor. Being hard of hearing can be funny because of some of the things she mishears.

There are even advantages to not hearing well. Hearing-impaired people can avoid loud noise by turning off their hearing aids. They need never listen to a bore. They develop good concentration because they are not distracted by outside noise. They can instantly have an oasis of quiet in any noisy situation.

Too many hard-of-hearing people still feel their disability is a stigma, as if it means they have lost their brains as well as their hearing or have been singled out for particular punishment. They try to hide what is essentially an invisible condition to begin with. This is encouraged by manufacturers' efforts to make ever smaller and more invisible hearing aids. "No one will know" is the message.

But why hide the fact that you don't hear well? Nora

has discovered that it is far more intelligent to let people know so they can help and so she can function far more successfully. Hearing aids come in bright colors now. Many small children love them; why not adults? And assistive devices are very visible. Nora wears a button saying "Hard of Hearing: Please Speak Clearly." She shows people she has a disability and is handling it to the best of her ability. She has taken responsibility for herself.

How do you know if you are hard of hearing? We mentioned a few things earlier in this chapter, but here's a quiz you can take. If any of your answers are "yes," maybe you should see a hearing care specialist.

1. Do you say "what?" a lot?
2. Do you ever have ringing in your ears?
3. Do you strain to hear over the phone?
4. Do you have trouble hearing when someone speaks to you from behind or from the next room?
5. Do you have trouble hearing in noisy group situations?
6. Do you sometimes misunderstand what people are saying, or miss jokes?
7. Do people say you turn up the TV too loud?
8. Do you turn your headphones up so loud you can't hear what people are saying?
9. Do you get ear infections often?
10. Is anyone in your family hearing-impaired?

If you think any of your family or friends and neighbors have a hearing loss, ask them to take this quiz too. It could lead to hearing better.

Nora remembers the time she went to the hardware store. She had paid for her purchase and the clerk said something she didn't catch. She asked politely for a repeat. Still no luck. Two more attempts, and then the clerk bellowed, "HAVE A NICE DAY, DAMMIT!" Everyone in the store, including Nora, laughed.

CHAPTER 9

WHAT HAPPENS WHEN YOU HAVE A HEARING TEST?

A hearing test should be routine, like a checkup at the dentist or the doctor. But maybe you're a little nervous, not knowing what to expect. For a start, where do you go? What are they going to do? Will it hurt? Will it take long? Are they going to work on you with strange machines? Who are "they" anyway? Let's find out what happens.

You will probably have a couple of choices of where to go: perhaps the hearing and speech center of your local hospital or clinic or an audiologist in private practice. If a local college or university has a speech and hearing training program they may also have an audiology clinic. There are also specialized centers like the New York League for the Hard of Hearing. The League, an independent agency, has the most extensive program on the east coast of the United States. Since 1910, it has provided a comprehensive program of rehabilitation, education, and counseling for infants, children and adults.

What is audiology and who is an audiologist? The words come from a mixture of the Latin "audire," to hear, and the Greek suffix "-ology," meaning "the study of." Audiologists are hearing health care professionals, have a master's or doctoral degree, and have taken science courses, including hearing and speech science, language and speech pathology, and anatomy and physiology. They will have studied computers and electronics and learned about rehabilitation and counseling. They apply their knowledge to helping hearing-impaired people make the best use of their sensory and oral skills to communicate effectively. Audiologists can also help people select hearing aids and assistive listening devices. In addition, they can test normally hearing people and teach them how best to preserve their hearing.

The American Speech-Language-Hearing Association (ASHA) certifies members of the profession; they earn a Certificate of Clinical Competency (CCC). Many states require audiologists to be licensed and currently registered by the state education department.

You've come to the clinic and met Ms. Wright, the audiologist. She is young and has a nice smile. She says you can call her Barbara and hopes you are not nervous. "It's not like a test you're going to get graded on—no one passes or fails around here. There are just things to listen to."

She takes you into the testing booth. It looks rather futuristic with soundproof walls (to keep out background noise), wires, headphones, and a window looking into the room where the audiologist has her equipment. You sit in a hi-tech seat that's surprisingly comfortable. The only odd notes are the kids' toys stacked in the corner. Barbara sees your eye caught by them and grins. "Not for you. They're to keep the little kids busy—and they are part of their testing equipment too." You now notice that they all have attached bells or rattles.

"Before we start doing anything," says Barbara, "let me tell you basically what all this is about. I am going to measure your hearing sensitivity by giving you different kinds of tests. First I'll check how loud a sound has to be for you to hear it and how soft before you can no longer hear it. I'll also test your speech discrimination—that's how clearly you hear words.

"While I am testing you, I'll make notations on this special chart called an *audiogram.* It's a visual way of indicating how well you hear."

You look at the chart, recognizing the decibel loudness levels entered on the left, vertical side, and the hertz frequencies, the pitch, going horizontally. (If you're not sure what they are, check back to Chapter 1.)

Barbara goes on, "The most important frequencies are between 500 and 2,000 hertz. That's where most of the sounds for understanding speech occur. A person with a hearing loss at all pitches generally has good word discrimination if they are said loudly enough. But if a person's loss is affected mainly in the higher pitches they will have greater difficulty understanding words because in English the less easily heard consonants are very important for speech. They can be responsible for up to 95 percent of the meaning of a word. It becomes hard to differentiate between words like "for*t*" and "for*ce,*" for example. And in a word like "kit" only the vowel sound might be heard.

"Let's start. I'll explain more as we go along."

Barbara puts the headphones over your ears, fixing them comfortably, and goes into the other room. You can see her through the window. You hear the click of the microphone as she switches it on.

"Can you hear me okay?" Her voice comes clearly through the mike. You nod.

"This machine is called a *pure tone audiometer.* It produces tones at different frequencies. We usually test at 250, 500, 1,000—up to 8,000 hertz. Each time you hear a sound, raise your hand." She winks reassuringly through the window. "Let's start on the right ear."

Every time you hear a beep you raise your hand. Some of the sounds are so soft you can't be sure you heard them at all, and that's what you tell Barbara. Some are high and

AUDIOLOGICAL EVALUATION

HEARING

71 WEST 23RD STREET, NEW YORK, NEW YORK 10010-4162
212-741-7650/TTY 212-255-1932

PATIENT'S NAME	
TEST DATE	BIRTHDATE
RELIABILITY	TEST METHOD
AUDIOLOGIST	AUDIOMETER

PURE TONE AUDIOMETRY (re ANSI 1969)

Hearing level in dB HL

FREQUENCY

-10 0 10 20 30 40 50 60 70 80 90 100 110

125 250 500 1000 2000 4000 8000

PTA

AIR	RIGHT	LEFT
BONE	RIGHT	LEFT

LEGEND

EAR	Air	Mask	Mastoid Bone Mask	Sound-field	Aided	FM Env. Tchr.	No Resp.
RIGHT	O	△	◁	☐		R	RE RT
LEFT	X	☐	▷	☐		L	LE LT
BINAURAL					S	B	BE BT

MASK.

| AIR | |
| BONE | |

	UNAIDED					AIDED						
	RIGHT	HL	LEFT	HL	SOUNDFIELD	HL	RIGHT	HL	LEFT	HL	BINAURAL	HL	COMMENTS
SAT		dB		dB		dB		dB		dB		dB	
SRT		dB		dB		dB		dB		dB		dB	
WORD RECOG.	%at	dB	%at	dB	%at	dB	%at	dB	%at	dB	%at	dB	
	%at	dB	%at	dB	%at	dB	%at	dB	%at	dB	%at	dB	
	%at	dB	%at	dB	%at	dB	%at	dB	%at	dB	%at	dB	
	%at	dB	%at	dB	%at	dB	%at	dB	%at	dB	%at	dB	
MCL		dB		dB		dB		dB		dB		dB	
UCL		dB		dB		dB		dB		dB		dB	
MATERIALS													

SPEECH AUDIOMETRY

TYMPANOGRAM

COMPLIANCE

MM H2O

-600 -500 -400 -300 -200 -100 0 100 200 300

ACOUSTIC REFLEX

STIMULUS RIGHT	CONTRALATERAL			STIMULUS LEFT			IPSILATERAL		
Reflex decay in 10 sec.	Threshold dB HL	HZ	Threshold dB HL	Reflex decay in 10 sec.		SPL	HZ	SPL
		500					500	
		1000					1000	
		2000						
		4000						

OTOSCOPIC

RIGHT

LEFT

COMMENTS

© 1985 NEW YORK LEAGUE FOR THE HARD OF HEARING

After a hearing evaluation, this blank form will be filled with the results of different tests. At the upper right is the audiogram chart.

loud so she only has to touch the button before your hand is up. She switches to your other ear and tests it the same way. She comes back into the booth and shows you what the audiogram looks like now:

Normal Hearing

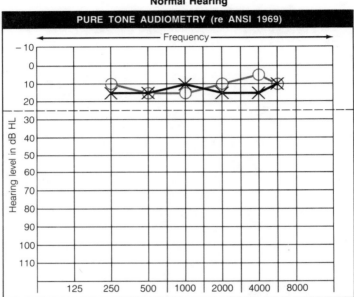

"Perfectly normal. We consider a response between 0 and 25 decibels normal and you are bang in the middle of the range. The circles represent your right ear, the crosses your left. When you hear the same in both ears, we just draw the crosses inside the circles. You could hear all the frequencies—pitches—starting from 250 hertz at 10 decibels; that's pretty soft, so you are in good shape."

You feel pleased and wonder what is coming next.

She removes the headphones and replaces them with a little unit that goes against the bone behind your ear. It is kept in place by a light metal band over your head.

98

"We just tested pure tone *air* conduction," Barbara says. "Now in this test we don't use your outer ear at all. I shall bypass it and go straight to your inner ear by using pure tone *bone* conduction. The gizmo behind your ear is an *oscillator*—it vibrates—and directly tests the sensitivity of your inner ear. Same beeps as before."

When Barbara comes back with the audiogram this time, it looks like this:

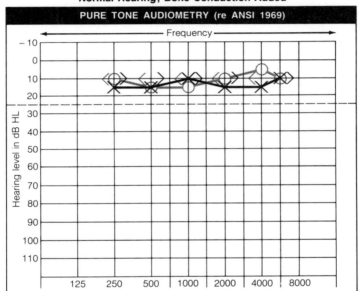

Normal Hearing; Bone Conduction Added

"The < > marks represent the bone conduction response: < for the right ear, > for the left. As you see, you can hear just as well when the sound goes *through* the outer ear to the inner ear as when it *bypasses* it to go straight to the inner ear." She adds some details to the chart. "Now you can see how you hear the sounds in the speech range:"

99

Normal Audiogram With Bone Conduction, With Speech Range Added

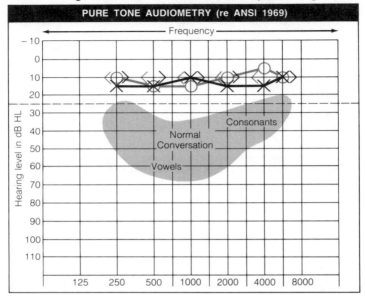

You like the way your chart looks. "What does it look like when someone has a hearing problem?" you ask.

"I can show you a couple of audiograms." Barbara comes back in a minute with the audiograms shown at right.

"The first two show a sensorineural loss. In fact they belong to the same person. The chart at the upper right shows the moderate sensorineural loss she had ten years ago when she first came here to be tested. Her left ear was slightly better than her right, but both are about the 45 to 65 decibel range. Ten years later it's a different story. The Os and Xs are now way down on the bottom chart. The sounds have to be very loud for her to hear them. The pure tone average is 90 to 100 decibels in both ears, a severe-to-profound, progressive hearing loss. The result is the same through air conduction and bone conduction. The outer/middle ear areas are okay. It's the nerve in the inner ear that's damaged.

100

Moderate Sensorineural Hearing Loss

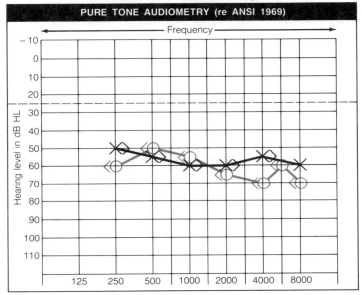

Audiogram Showing Severe-to-Profound Sensorineural Hearing Loss

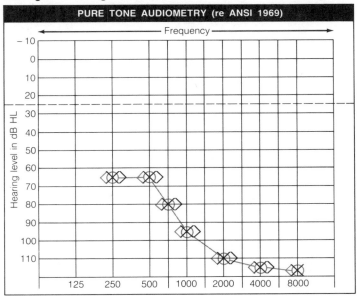

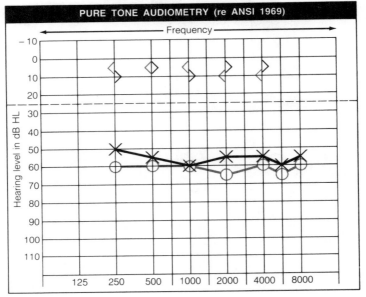

Moderate Conductive Hearing Loss

PURE TONE AUDIOMETRY (re ANSI 1969)

"The audiogram above shows someone with a conductive loss. The hearing level was okay when sound bypassed the outer ear, so the inner ear was working properly, but the person needed quite a high decibel level to hear through the headphones. Something in the outer part of the middle ear was preventing sound from getting through. This is a case when medical treatment or surgery might be able to remove the obstruction, and the person's hearing would improve.

"Okay, let's do the second half of the testing. The headphones go back on for this. I'm going to test how well you hear speech. I shall cover my face so it's ears only—no visual clues. The first is a *speech reception threshold* test. I'll say some familiar two-syllable words that have the same emphasis on both syllables, starting loud and getting softer and softer down the decibel levels. You keep raising your hand as you hear the words. Ready? Cowboy . . . hot dog . . . airplane . . . sidewalk . . .''

You don't need to see her face. You raise your hand at each word as they get fainter and fainter.

"Great," says Barbara. "Now the last test. I'll say a list of single-syllable words and I want you to repeat each one after me. Again, ears only. This is called a *speech discrimination* test and checks if you can hear the different vowel and consonant sounds making up a familiar word. You shouldn't have any trouble at all. I'll say the words at normal speech level. Boat . . . call . . . pin . . . sat . . .''

Barbara is right. You score one hundred percent. She tells you, "A hearing-impaired person may get a very low score on both these tests. This doesn't mean they've 'failed' the tests or are stupid. It simply shows what they can or cannot hear.

"Thank you for coming. Tell your friends to come, too. Here's a photocopy of your audiogram; you might want to show it to them. Steer clear of noise!''

You put the audiogram in your pocket, say good-bye, and run down the steps outside. You feel good. It didn't hurt. It only took about half an hour and it was really quite interesting. You forgot to ask Barbara if you could look at the equipment on her side of the window. Next time. And the best thing of all is that you know your hearing is fine.

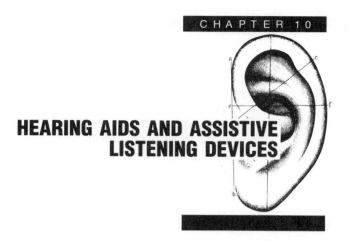

CHAPTER 10

HEARING AIDS AND ASSISTIVE LISTENING DEVICES

Hearing aids have not been around very long. How did people manage before they were invented? Not well. They cupped their hands around their ears to funnel sound. They asked people to speak louder. And they got left out a lot, often becoming completely isolated. By the eighteenth century people were using ear trumpets and speaking tubes which funneled and concentrated sound into the ear. Some people had special gadgets made. A nineteenth-century catalog offered trumpets hidden in hats, fans, canes, umbrellas, and other accessories. One, worn under the chin, could be concealed by a beard or scarf. Also last century, King Goa VI of Portugal had ear trumpets fitted into the armrests of his throne. Manufacturers experimented with other kinds of ''hearing chairs.''

In 1872 Alexander Graham Bell invented the first real hearing aid, an electrical one for his deaf mother. But electrical hearing aids only became commercially available early in this century. They were bulky, made up of several wire-connected parts carried on the body.

A major breakthrough followed the invention of the transistor in 1947. Transistorized hearing aids appeared commercially in the early 1950s. They were much smaller, used one battery instead of two, and—for better or worse—allowed the wearer largely to conceal the hearing loss.

As technology advanced, hearing aids became even smaller. The electronic circuitry is now micro-etched onto a silicon chip, a truly miniaturized amplifying system. Aids are now becoming more sophisticated acoustically. Until recently it was a case of "one aid fits all;" now a certain amount of individual fitting is possible.

A hearing aid is made up of these components:

- a *microphone* that picks up sound waves
- an *amplifier* that makes the sound louder
- a *receiver* (like a loudspeaker) to deliver the louder sound to the ear
- a *battery* that provides the power to operate the aid
- an *ear mold* that connects the aid to the ear

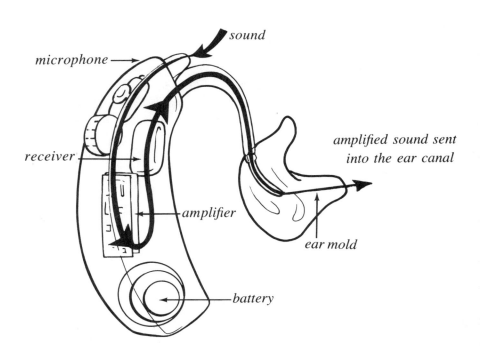

105

Other features include the *volume control,* which is set into the back of the aid casing and allows adjustment to louder and quieter listening situations.

The *on-off switch* is set into a little panel also on the back of the aid casing. An extra feature of this panel is the *T-switch,* (T for telephone). An aid with a T-switch contains magnetic coils that pick up signals from telephones fitted with a special inductive coupler. All phones manufactured in the United States must now be hearing-aid compatible in this way. The T-switch can be used with many of the assistive listening devices described later in this chapter.

Some aids have direct *audio input jacks* for plugging in radios, tape recorders, or a microphone.

A hearing aid for one ear is monaural; two aids, one for each ear, are binaural.

There are basically five types of hearing aids: behind the ear, in the ear, body aids, eyeglass aids and crossover (CROS) aids.

Behind-the-ear aids. Everything is in one unit that fits snugly over and behind the ear. The plastic case, an inch or an inch-and-a-half long, is connected by clear plastic tubing to the ear mold that fits inside the ear. Behind-the-ear aids are suitable for all levels of hearing loss.

In-the-ear aids are becoming increasingly popular. Everything is in one customized unit, made to fit a particular person's outer ear and ear canal shape. These aids are for mild to moderate losses. They are so small they do not have room for a T-switch and are difficult to manage if a person's hands are not deft, so some have remote controls. Canal aids are an even smaller version of in-the-ear aids, also for mild to moderate losses, and definitely require manual dexterity.

Eyeglass hearing aids. As the name implies, the parts of the aid are built into the frame of the glasses. Tubing connects the ear mold to the aid. Eyeglass aids or a cord connecting two behind-the-ear aids can be used for the

106

CROS fitting, which stands for the rather pompous term "Contralateral Routing of Signals." It means that if a person has a severe loss, but only in one ear, the sound can be routed from a microphone near the impaired ear across to the good ear.

Eyeglass aids are like behind-the ear aids except that the parts are contained in the frames of the glasses.

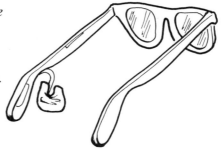

Body hearing aids. These are used mainly by people with profound hearing loss because the microphone, amplifier, and battery are larger and more powerful. A body aid is encased in a small flat box that can be clipped to a shirt pocket or belt. A cord connects the box to the receiver "button" at ear level, which is in turn connected to the ear mold.

In hearing aids like this, the microphone, amplifier, and batteries are in a rectangular case that clips to the body. A cord connects the case to the receiver in the ear mold.

107

One other kind of aid is for *bone conduction* loss. This is placed behind the ear in the way it was in the hearing test described in the last chapter. It channels sound through the bone of the skull, sending the vibrations directly to the inner ear.

It is worth noting that not everyone can be helped by a hearing aid. Hearing aids do not restore normal hearing, unlike glasses that can correct vision to 20/20 normality. Hearing aids make sounds louder and can bring some sounds back into hearing range. They do not clarify speech. In fact the sound that comes through the aids is not that of normal speech. Because aids are electronic, the sound can be somewhat metallic and harsh. Aids are being improved, rather slowly, as technology advances.

Digital aids are the "new breed" of hearing aids. They are already being tailored through computer technology to meet individual needs to a certain extent and can filter out some of the competing background noise that makes understanding speech so difficult, for example, air conditioners and traffic, although not yet the human voice. The aim is to produce a hearing aid that does this well enough to allow a hearing-impaired person to communicate as normally as possible. Researchers are working on more accurate ways of diagnosing and testing a person's hearing in order to find the best combination of mathematical formulas for individually programming a digital aid.

These in-the-works digital aids are actually computers-in-the-ear. Microprocessor chips alter and enhance sounds, especially those in the speech range. The amplification is matched exactly to a person's hearing loss. The aid will also cut out background noise and *feedback* (whistling or squealing in the aid). Whenever there is a change in environmental sound, the computer will immediately make the necessary changes in the hearing aid, as directed by the particular program. The aid will be upgradable as technology changes, and the software can be reprogrammed as the person's hearing alters over time. The chief challenges are the size of the aid, because it needs a larger energy/power unit, and the cost. It will be expensive.

Hearing aids are already expensive, and many otherwise comprehensive insurance companies do not cover the cost of them. Whatever the method of payment, when a person decides to acquire one—an aid should last from three to five years—the fitting should be done by a qualified professional: an audiologist or licensed hearing aid dealer/dispenser.

Very few people can walk out of the office with their new aids and function successfully right away. A period of adjustment and learning is part of the hearing aid evaluation process. The dispenser will tell the client what to expect, what is possible, and what isn't. The client may have to try several aids before deciding which is best for him or her. The dispenser explains how the aid works and how to get used to it. This includes looking after the aid, changing the batteries, and making sure the ear mold fits comfortably.

An *ear mold* is made of a plastic or hypoallergenic material and custom-molded for the individual person's ear. Inserted fairly tightly into the ear canal, it is connected to the aid by tubing, and, as well as directing sound inward, helps keep the aid in place. If it is too tight, it may make the ear sore. If it is too loose, sound can leak back into the aid causing feedback (whistling). A problem is that often the wearer can't hear the feedback to correct it and has to be told.

There are not yet any real miracles in hearing aids. But one new technology is something like a miracle in helping some profoundly deaf people have basic hearing again. This is the "electronic ear"—the *cochlear implant*. Since the first implant in 1970, over 3,000 people have received them, from very young children to the elderly.

The pre-requirements until fairly recently for a cochlear implant have been postlingual deafness (in most cases) and a profound loss in both ears that cannot be helped by hearing aids. Also, a large enough area of the auditory nerve must be intact because it is the nerve, not the useless, damaged, cochlear hair cells, that will be electrically stimulated.

Prelingually deaf adults are rarely given cochlear implants: if hearing aids cannot help them, an implant probably won't. But now, increasingly, prelingually deaf children are receiving implants.

Cochlear implants use electrodes—"channels"—placed in the inner ear to stimulate the auditory nerve. The earliest devices had one channel. The newer ones have twenty-two, each programmed individually, which means a wider range of sounds reach the auditory nerve. The brain can then decode them for meaning.

People who have an implant can hear medium to loud sounds, their own voices, and have an improved means of communication, together with lipreading—and sometimes even without it. Many can use the telephone. A cochlear implant costs between $6,000 and $10,000, which is already a lot less than the early implants. The device is being further developed. Maybe miracles *can* occur with the help of technology.

Assistive Listening Devices (ALDs) are also relatively new on the scene. Just ten years ago hearing aids were the only devices available. If people couldn't hear on the phone, they didn't use the phone and depended unwillingly on others to make essential calls for them. If they could literally only watch television, that's all they did. They missed a great deal at school, at work, and even when just trying to enjoy themselves.

ALDs help to loosen the grip of hearing loss.

As you have seen, laws now mandate hearing help in many public places and modes of communication. The telephone is one of these. Hearing-aid-compatible phones are identified by the blue plastic grommet—protective ma-

110

terial—where the cable joins the handset. The telephone was invented by Alexander Graham Bell, whose wife, like his mother, was deaf. Ironically, the phone has turned out to be the chief obstacle for the hearing impaired. Phone communication can, however, be amplified by a volume control in the handset or a portable amplifier that can be slipped over the earpiece. Using the T-switch with the phone cuts out much background noise.

Those who cannot use a regular phone can still telephone by TDD—a *T*elecommunications *D*evice for the *D*eaf. (Early versions were teletypewriters called TTYs.) A TDD is a typewriter-like machine with a one- or two-line read-out display. The handset of the phone fits into a coupler/modem of two rubberized cups. You communicate over the regular phone lines with someone else who has a TDD. You dial in the ordinary way, but instead of speaking and listening, both callers place the handset in the coupler cups and they type their conversation. An added printer can provide a record of it. TDDs can also be made computer compatible; hearing-impaired people should have the same access to computer information networks as hearing people. Conversely, a personal computer can often be equipped with a special modem so it can work as a TDD. A basic TDD costs about $150; the price increases as options such as answering machine capabilities are added.

In several states TDD users can also communicate with hearing people, and vice versa, through a *relay system* that operates twenty-four hours a day every day. The hearing-impaired person calls a toll-free number on the TDD and a hearing "third party" operator using a TDD links the deaf person with the hearing person by relaying spoken messages one way and typed messages the other. The calls are charged in the usual way. While the relay is currently only statewide and only in certain states, it is hoped that soon it will be nationwide—and one day worldwide as well.

Many federal and state agencies, police, hospitals, and fire departments and a host of businesses and other com-

111

A girl learns how to operate a TDD. Once she masters it, she will be able to communicate by phone with many hearing and hearing-impaired people.

mercial enterprises have TDDs now. The International Directory for TDD Users grows thicker each year. TDDs and relays are slowly freeing the hearing impaired to communicate over the phone like everyone else.

How do you know the phone is ringing if you can't hear it even with a loud bell? A whole range of *visual alerting devices* can be set up in your home. You can have lights that flash when the phone or doorbell rings, the baby cries, the smoke alarm is activated, the wake-up alarm goes off. (If you prefer, or will sleep through a light flashing, you can connect a vibrator to the alarm clock. This "bed-shaker" can be put under the mattress or pillow and is guaranteed to wake even Rip Van Winkle.) Many hotels now have visual alerting systems for hearing-impaired guests.

There are also driving aids. One is a loud beeper that reminds the driver to switch off a turn signal unintentionally left on because the driver can't hear the clicking. Police or ambulance sirens can activate a warning light on the dash.

Hearing as well as watching television has long been on the want list of deaf people. Now *telecaptioning decoders* let people read subtitles of television dialogue on hundreds of hours of TV programming a week. Simultaneous "real time" captioning of live events is also increasing. These "closed" captions are not visible without a decoder. Decoders are occasionally built into the set—in the future they all will be—but currently you have to buy a separate one. A TEXT channel gives news, sports, news of interest to the hearing impaired, and television program listings. Decoders cost under $200. The latest is cable ready. You can connect it to any TV, cable TV hookup, and satellite receiver or VCR. Captioning is shown in regular TV listings by "CC" (Closed Captioning) or , the symbol of the National Captioning Institute. See if you can find it in the newspaper or programming guide.

GOOD EVENING. I'M PETER JENNINGS.

The National Captioning Institute captions more than 375 hours of network and cable programming a week.

Movies have also been off limits to the hearing impaired, except for foreign films with subtitles. Captioned Films for the Deaf, funded by the government, is in the forefront of captioning English-language movies. Movies for VCRs are captioned about six months after they first appear. These are "open" captions; no decoder is needed.

Face-to-face communication is often a major difficulty for hearing-impaired people, especially in group situations (large and small) and noisy places like restaurants. There are several types of alternative listening systems that many people find helpful in these situations:

- induction/audio loops
- AM systems
- FM systems
- infrared systems

Audio loop. A microphone sends sound through an amplifier to an insulated wire "loop" which is placed around the large or small listening area and plugged into an electrical outlet. The listeners must be inside the "magic circle." The magnetic field created by the current passing through the loop can be picked up by a hearing aid T-switch or a hand-held receiver with an ear piece. The speaker must talk into the microphone to be heard.

AM systems are the cheapest to use and do not require a hearing aid. Sound is transmitted over an AM radio wavelength and received through a personal headset or portable radio.

FM (frequency modulation) systems, already mentioned several times, are also a radio link between speaker and listener, but FM systems have much better sound quality. The speaker has a microphone either hand-held or attached by a clip to blouse or jacket so that the source of the sound, the voice, is close to the mike. The sound is transmitted over a special FM frequency to a personal receiver worn by the listener, attached to a belt or stashed in a pocket. The receiver directs the sound signals to the ears

115

by a headphone (no hearing aid necessary), a direct audio input unit attached by a "boot" to the hearing aid(s), or a mini-loop worn around the neck with the aid on the T-switch.

The listener using an FM system can be a couple of hundred feet from the speaker or across the table, indoors or out, in quiet or noisy situations, or in small or large groups. The system, originally designed for the classroom, is naturally popular with the hearing impaired, and, although expensive, is worth it for the freedom it offers.

Perhaps the truest sound is found in *infrared systems.* These use invisible and harmless infrared light waves. Sound is converted into infrared light signals and transmitted to a receiver worn by the listener, where it is turned back into sound. The battery-powered receiver hangs down from the ears rather like a doctor's stethoscope and is used instead of hearing aids. The system can also be used with a T-switch and a neck loop. Infrared is often used in the theater and in concert halls, but it can also be easily set up in the home for use in conversation or for TV. Unfortunately it can't be used outside because the sun interferes with the transmission, and it is only good for mild to moderate hearing losses. Again it is fairly expensive. There are no cheap options for the hearing impaired! If a person is skilled electronically or knows someone who is an electrician, home-made systems can sometimes be put together less expensively.

CHAPTER 11

HEARING EAR DOGS

At 7:30 A.M. Michael's alarm clock jumps on his bed to wake him. The alarm clock has a cold nose and furry ears. . . .

It is his hearing dog, Biscuit. A mixed breed sheltie, Biscuit is not only an "alarm clock"; she alerts Michael, who is deaf, to a variety of sounds—sounds the hearing person takes for granted because they are part of everyday life—the doorbell or phone, for example, or warnings of danger like a smoke alarm.

Biscuit is a trained, certified hearing dog (also known as a hearing ear dog or a guide dog for the deaf). Since training programs began less than fifteen years ago, dogs like Biscuit have proved essential to more than 3,000 hearing-impaired people. Along the way—like Seeing Eye dogs—they have become a symbol of the owner's disability. Hearing dogs are even more of a visible symbol, pointing up the invisible handicap of deafness.

In the United States today there are approximately thirty-five ongoing training programs for hearing dogs. The American Humane Association began the first program in 1976, setting up guidelines and criteria. Demand quickly outstripped supply, and programs were started across the country. Now entitled The American Humane Associa-

117

tion/Delta Society Hearing Dog Resource Center, the Association no longer trains dogs, but acts as a source of referral and information.

One of the training programs is Red Acre Farm Hearing Dog Center in Stow, Massachusetts. (Others are listed at the back of this book.) A not-for-profit institution started in 1981 and serving forty-three states, Red Acre Farm's program is fairly typical. All hearing dog programs have the same goal: To supply a hearing-impaired person with a useful and compatible hearing dog, but methods of training vary at different centers.

Red Acre Farm is on a hilly, wooded lane in quiet Stow, midway between Worcester and Boston. The first sight you might see is a volunteer walking a willing, tail-wagging "student" dog from the white wooden kennel building to the main house for a training session. The staff of eight includes the program director, the two dog trainers, and the "people trainers." Volunteers round out the team. The staff members have degrees in education and are strong in sign language, which is the primary language of many clients. The first question you get at Red Acre Farm is, "Do you find it easier to sign or speak?" paving the way courteously for a relaxed visit. The program specializes in one-on-one training; there are no group sessions.

Twelve to fourteen dogs are trained a year. They are mostly abandoned, homeless dogs that have been placed in animal shelters where they confront the possibility of death because of overcrowded facilities. So two good deeds are achieved in one stroke: A dog's life is saved—many hundreds of lives a year, all told—and a human being is helped. Red Acre Farm acquires most of its dogs from the Animal Rescue League in Boston.

Not every dog can be a hearing ear dog. In fact, only a quarter of those considered are accepted for training. The qualities trainers look for are a friendly, steady character; curiosity, especially about sound; intelligence; age (eight to fourteen months); general health; and a willingness to learn and work—a hearing dog is on duty around the clock. And of course the dog must have good hearing. Red Acre Farm has found that one of the best kinds of dog is a medium-sized mixed breed like Hatti, one of the Center's five Demonstration Dogs, owned by a hearing trainer. Hatti is an outgoing, bright, six-year-old, very sound aware, who obviously loves her work. She even talks into the telephone when requested.

Once a dog is chosen, has been spayed or neutered, and has had its shots, it goes into a quarantine kennel for two weeks at Red Acre Farm—for added health safety precautions. It then goes to the main kennel to start training. Part of the kennel, divided into six indoor/outdoor sections, is home to eager, bouncy, young dogs in training. Beyond, leashes hang in a row on the wall. A couple of cats are comfortably asleep. A trainer picks up three dog carriers from shelves in the entrance; she is off to Boston to collect new dogs.

The first formal training is conventional. The dog is taught house manners and general obedience: To "heel," "come," "sit," "down," and "stay" by voice and gesture. Many deaf people do not speak, so the dog must be trained to obey gestured commands. Positive reinforcement is the training method—that is, reward by food and petting when the dog does something correctly. (The food reward is gradually phased out.)

The rest of the program is designed to help hearing-impaired people cope with some of the practical difficulties of their disability. In a homelike setting the dogs learn to recognize, and respond to basic sounds in a household and in daily life by physical contact with the owner. These are sounds the deaf person can't hear in a world built around sound. They include the alarm clock, doorbell, telephone, teakettle whistle, smoke and fire alarm, baby cry, and someone calling the person's name. The alarm is taught first because it is the easiest to learn. As you saw with

119

Michael, the dog jumps onto the bed and walks over him or licks his face until he responds. Most hearing dogs are small or medium in size because they are easier to care for. A larger dog will nudge or lick from the side of the bed. As Ellen Terryberry, program director at Red Acre Farm, says, "Fifty pounds of dog jumping on you in the morning would definitely be a rude awakening!"

For most sounds, the dog goes to the owner, gets his attention, takes him to the source of the sound (the phone, for example), and stays there until told it's okay to move. The exception to this rule is the smoke/fire alarm. The dog alerts the owner and then lies down. It would be dangerous in this case to go to the source of the sound because that's where the fire is.

The dog can also be trained to work in other environments such as the owner's workplace.

So far, Red Acre Farm has not accepted household pets for training. There is too much *un*training and *re*training to do. But recently they worked with a privately owned dog. Both dog and owner passed the strict screening for acceptance into the program.

Training takes four to six months and much patience before a dog is ready to be matched with an owner. Many kinds of people use hearing dogs; some are those with acquired deafness who don't sign; some live alone or with other hearing-impaired people where there is no other dog in the house. Other people are born deaf, maybe young professionals living by themselves or with a roommate, or deaf parents with young hearing children, or older people who want to stay independent. A hearing dog makes a social difference as well as an assistive one, improving personal relationships and bringing isolated people in contact with others.

A hearing ear dog can alert a deaf mother to the cries of her baby.

Just as not every dog will make a good hearing ear dog, not every person is a suitable owner. An applicant must be emotionally, physically, and financially able to undertake a relationship which might mean a commitment for many years. And he or she must be realistic about a dog's capabilities.

The applicant sends in an audiogram, references, and a detailed application form giving health history and the kind of home environment the dog will live in. The person then comes to Red Acre Farm to be interviewed or is interviewed by a regional representative if distance is prohibitive.

Once a client is accepted and matched with a dog, the dog has to be trained to the client's specific needs. But the client has to learn obedience training too. Staying at Red Acre Farm for a week of intensive training, the client learns from a placement counselor how to take care of the dog and how to respond when alerted to a sound. The person must be able to adjust to changes in life-style and allow the dog to work. That means letting the dog respond to sounds at all times and not letting, say, hearing visitors intervene or take over. Most important is the transfer of the dog's obedience from trainer to new owner; a new bond must be forged.

After this week the dog goes to its new home to begin a second week of training in the new environment under the supervision of a staff member who helps the client provide a smooth transition. The same sound sources the dog has been trained to respond to are in use, but the surroundings are different, and there may be family, friends, and neighbors to get acquainted with. The placement counselor helps with dog care and house manners, such as no dogs on furniture unless on duty. And she makes both of them practice.

After three months of satisfactory performance by both dog and client, supervised by a representative, ownership is transferred and certification is granted. A diploma is presented on "graduation." The owner gets an ID card with a photo of the dog, certifying that the dog has been trained by Red Acre Farm. This information is on the reverse of the card:

This is a Hearing Dog trained to alert the bearer to specific sounds and registered with the Red Acre Farm Hearing Dog Program. The hearing impaired card-holder is trained in performance standards and obedience responsibility. This card pictures a dog professionally trained in auditory awareness and requests a passage permit for the Hearing Dog to accompany its hearing-impaired master on all airlines and public transportation, in all public facilities and in all forms of housing.

Hearing dogs and their owners are guaranteed equal access by law into public facilities, public housing, and on public transportation throughout the United States. They have the same rights and privileges as guide dogs for the blind. In New York State, Article 7B of Law 47 declares the legal status of hearing dogs. It is wise to carry a photocopy of this civil rights legislation because places like restaurants often object if you bring in a dog. Of course the dog must behave properly.

Working dogs can be identified by their bright orange or yellow collars and leashes, often with the name of their training center printed on them.

What does a hearing dog cost? Training a hearing dog runs to about $3,500. Red Acre Farm does not charge the client. Obviously, if clients can pay for their dog, they do, but dogs can be sponsored by various other sources or through fundraising grants from clubs like the Lions or Kiwanis. The National Theatre of the Deaf performs an annual benefit for Red Acre Farm. An owner must, however, be financially able to look after a dog.

Why not simply invest in some assistive listening de-

Hearing ear dogs and their owners should not be subject to discrimination. They must be allowed into public housing and onto public transportation.

vices? They're far less bother than a living dog. But while the hearing impaired can, and do, use these devices, a flashing light bulb doesn't respond to a hug or give total and selfless affection.

In clinical terms, a hearing dog has therapeutic value, helping hearing-impaired people conquer depression and providing companionship, security, peace of mind, and independence. But this evaluation does not begin to describe the bond that develops between dog and owner. The person has "ears" again through the dog; the world reopens to sounds. The person still can't hear them, but the dog alerts him or her to the fact that they are there. Many dogs go beyond their formal training, alerting their owners to any unusual sound, from the simple dropping of a bunch of keys to making them aware of unheard danger. One hearing dog persuaded his owner to leave a bus. Outside she saw the the whole roof of the bus was on fire.

Perhaps what a hearing dog means is most poignantly told by Hannah Merker, a writer who lives on a houseboat in Long Island Sound:

We have been separated only once . . . when Sheena spent a week in the hospital. A car was speeding down the harbor road by our boat yard. My mind elsewhere, I did not notice Sheena's signals. Nor did I hear the warning shouts of nearby people. Sheena threw herself between me and the oncoming car.

Sheena recovered and is still Hannah's ears. Hannah says, "I am touching the world again, a world so many take for granted, the world of sound."

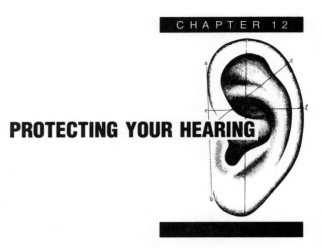

CHAPTER 12

PROTECTING YOUR HEARING

How tough are your ears? They seem to be pretty resilient, considering the many hours of abuse they take each day in our noisy world. You might even think they simply get used to noise. But constant exposure to noise doesn't toughen your ears the way exercise toughens your muscles. It's just the opposite. The noisier the environment and the longer your exposure, the more likely you are to damage your hearing.

When does sound become noise and at what point is noise too much? Take a look again at the decibel chart in Chapter 1. There you can see the intensity *level* at which sound becomes damaging. But damage is also caused by *how long* you are exposed to a sound. The table at right will give you some idea of how long you can safely listen to your stereo headset, for example, at different decibel levels.

You can see that the lower the decibel level, the longer you can listen safely.

Noise can further be described as transient or continuous. Short bursts of sound are *transient*—a door slamming, a gunshot. Exposure to 115 decibels for fifteen minutes a day—for a commuter in a major city subway car, for example—will eventually cause hearing loss. *Continu-*

126

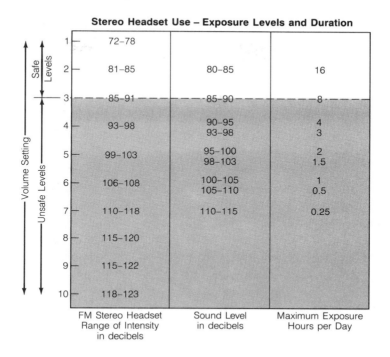

Stereo Headset Use – Exposure Levels and Duration

Volume Setting		FM Stereo Headset Range of Intensity in decibels	Sound Level in decibels	Maximum Exposure Hours per Day
Safe Levels	1	72–78		
	2	81–85	80–85	16
	3	85–91	85–90	8
Unsafe Levels	4	93–98	90–95 / 93–98	4 / 3
	5	99–103	95–100 / 98–103	2 / 1.5
	6	106–108	100–105 / 105–110	1 / 0.5
	7	110–118	110–115	0.25
	8	115–120		
	9	115–122		
	10	118–123		

ous noise is an ongoing succession of sounds, like the repetitive hammering of machinery or the whine of a chainsaw. Exposure to continuous noise of over 85 decibels for eight hours daily will eventually harm your hearing. For example, a waiter working in a noisy, clattering restaurant is at risk.

The chief enemy of hearing is noise. It's a noisy world around us. Trucks and buses rumble by, police and ambulance sirens blast, horns honk, dogs bark, radios blare, airplanes thunder overhead, subway trains roar underground. In the country, in backyards, in some workplaces, machinery and power tools whirr, bang, and clank. Even our homes are invaded by noise pollution: vacuum cleaners, blenders, air conditioners, stereo systems . . . .

How do you know when something is too loud and therefore dangerous? You can keep the decibel chart in mind, and there are also ways that your ears warn you. A noise is dangerously loud if:

- You have to shout to be heard above it
- Your ears buzz or ring for several hours afterward
- You have pain in your ears from it
- Sounds seem muffled and you have to strain to hear normally for some time afterward

If you have any of these symptoms, don't ignore them. Tell your parents, go to your school nurse, have your hearing checked. And avoid the noisy situations.

The trouble is that hearing damage is usually subtle and insidious. You look the same, you feel the same, and you may not become conscious of the damage for years. But the damage has been done. And if your hearing is damaged there is at present no cure.

In the future science may well be able to replace damaged ear parts or ears. Cochlear implants are already helping some people. Hearing aids and ALDs help once hearing becomes impaired. But why allow the damage to happen in the first place? Why take chances with such a valuable part of you? You've read about the difficulties facing the hearing impaired. There are some things you can do to prevent them, to a large extent, from happening to you. Prevention—in the case of hearing problems more than in many other things—is far more effective than attempts at cure.

There are many sources of environmental noise pollution that we cannot individually control. But we can reduce or avoid at least some of it. You can, for example, turn down the volume of your personal stereo headset. Too much listening to loud music, even if it is your favorite group or soloist, can damage your hearing. Quieter music also gives you the bonus of hearing the details, words, and background more clearly.

At a rock concert or a noisy sports event, where the decibel level can exceed 120 decibels, you can at least put your fingers in your ears. Much more effective: Wear earplugs or earmuffs. They look like headphones so no one will know that they are earplugs. Anyway it's not "wimpy" to wear ear protection; ground technicians at airports wear them and making sure that jets take off and land safely is anything but a wimpy job. Earplugs and earmuffs won't interfere with your fun, and they will reduce the amount of noise entering your ears. Try to limit the time you spend at noisy events. Though jet planes (and automobiles) are quieter than those built in the 1960s and 1970s, they are still dangerously noisy. Rabbits living around Dulles Airport in Washington, D.C., are deaf—and now produce a new breed of deaf rabbits. Human ears are no tougher.

Remember that motorbikes, motorboats, water jetskis, and off-road-vehicles such as snowmobiles also operate at dangerously high levels of noise. And forget all about "boom" cars filled with multiple speakers, amplifiers and compact discs producing all kinds of window-shattering music at up to 150 decibels. Thunder on wheels is the quick route to total silence.

Your family can "noiseproof" your home. Hard surfaces amplify sound: tile or stone floors, unadorned walls, uncurtained windows . . . Absorb sound by using rugs, carpets, drapes, and cushioned furniture. Stand noisy appliances like washing machines and mixers on sound-absorbing mats instead of the bare floor or counter.

Hearing loss is expected to increase in the general population. The National Institute on Aging projects that a quarter of the population age thirty-five to forty-four and three-quarters of those aged forty-five to fifty-four will suffer hearing loss in the next thirty years!

Campaign against excessive noise. It's in your own interest. People are becoming hearing impaired at a younger and younger age, and noise is one of the chief culprits. Doctors and audiologists say they are seeing more and more teenagers whose audiograms would be more typical of senior citizens. "SHHHerman" can help you campaign. He's the "lion who doesn't roar," and he appears on posters showing ways to "tame" noise. "Noise can be beastly," he says. SHHHerman is part of an educational and outreach program; you can learn more about his work by writing to the address at the back of this book.

You can ask your social sciences teacher to show movies and videos about noise pollution and hearing conservation in class. Some sources are given at the back of the book. Many movies are available free or for a small fee. Your local library may also have a loan service you can use. If they don't have the videos themselves, they can get them for you. Environmental noise control is under the jurisdiction of the Environmental Protection Agency, and most cities have local noise regulations. You should know what they are in your city or town.

Noise is not a new problem. Before the rubber tires of cars, iron-shod horses pulling iron-wheeled carriages clattered over cobblestoned streets. And steam trains would have drowned out diesel or electric trains. The blacksmith's anvil rang with each blow of the hammer. Industrial noise goes back to the eighteenth century and earlier. Workers hammering copper as a trade "have their ears so injured by the perpetual din," said a contemporary, "that . . . they become hard of hearing and, if they grow old at this work, completely deaf." Millers "in the constant noise of wheels and millstones and the roar of water . . . are nearly always hard of hearing."

The nineteenth-century industrial revolution was responsible for a marked increase in industrial deafness; boilermakers, cotton mill workers, and others in the newly developed branches of heavy industry were victims of progress. Noise in industry today, and in the workplace in general, continues to rise and to affect people. Jobs with built-in noise include shipbuilding, mining, printing, and food processing. The number of people affected and the

NOISE CAN BE BEASTLY.

DECIBELS:

140 Firecrackers, an air raid siren, gunshot blast

130 Jackhammer, live rock music

120 Jet plane taking off, a basketball game in a gym

110 Shouting in someone's ear, a race car

100 Garbage truck, a snowmobile

90 Motorcycle, a powermower, a heavy truck

80 Alarm clock, a hair dryer, a vacuum cleaner

70 City or freeway traffic

60 Normal conversation, a room air-conditioner

50 Rainfall, a refrigerator

40 The principal's office, leaves rustling

30 Library, a soft whisper

Use your head. Keep your hearing.

OPERATION:
SHHH

amount of hearing loss depends on the kind of work; factory noise differs from office noise, for example. And the rate of deterioration depends on the noise level, the length of time a person is exposed, and its cumulative effect; it builds up over time.

Laws regulate the permissible noise level in the workplace: Noise must be reduced to the lowest level practicable. Pursuant to the Occupational Safety and Health Act (OSHA) of 1970, regulations were amended in 1983 governing noise control and hearing conservation in general industry. If noise exceeds safety levels—a maximum of 90 decibels for an eight-hour workday—structural changes may have to be made to buildings or work schedules may have to be altered to decrease the length of time workers are exposed. Workers should use ear protectors, when using jackhammers to repair the street, for instance, and should have their hearing monitored and tested periodically.

Trade unions work for safe conditions for their members, but employees are also responsible for themselves. They must speak up for safer hearing conditions and use hearing protection. They have to remember that ears don't build up immunity to noise.

There is another, new, way to block out unwanted sound: *antinoise*. Noise is a wave of pressure traveling through the air. Antinoise is its mirror image—an equal but opposite wave. When noise meets antinoise they cancel each other out, leaving quiet. The antinoise wave is generated digitally or by analog. Sounds that are still needed, the human voice, for example, can be retained through computer manipulations. At present, only low-pitched sounds can be successfully eliminated, but as the technology develops almost any unwanted noise will be removable.

Noise does not only affect your hearing. It can make you feel tired, produce anxiety, stress, and high blood pressure. It can even cause nervous breakdowns and violent behavior.

132

Although it is the most important factor, noise is not the only danger to your hearing that you can correct. You can take care of your hearing health in other ways. If you have an earache or an ear infection, go to a doctor immediately and avoid swimming until you know what the cause is. Sports and recreation are sometimes hazardous for ears. When you are swimming or surfing, watch for water in your ears. Water can encourage fungus growth and ear infections like swimmer's ear (external otitis). If your ear feels itchy, use dry-out drops. If itching persists, or the ear is sore or swollen, see a doctor. When doing any winter sports cover your ears with a hat or earmuffs to guard against frostbite. In boxing, the ear is at risk from blows. And deep sea divers must take special precautions against the effects of water pressure.

Make sure that in your annual health checkup the doctor also checks your ears. Don't poke anything in your ear; a punctured eardrum increases chances of infection and hearing problems.

Some drugs are known to be *ototoxic,* bad for the ears (literally, poison, from the Greek word "toxicon," and from the Greek "otos," for ear). Ototoxic drugs include some members of the mycin group of antibiotics. Aspirin and quinine taken in large quantities can affect your hearing, at the least producing tinnitus. Hearing loss due to use of these substances, however, is reversible; if you stop taking them your hearing will return to normal, one of the few cases where this occurs.

Alcohol abuse can also affect your hearing. When a person is drunk, the ears do not register noise as too loud until a much higher noise level is reached. This is another very good reason not to start drinking.

Many researchers think that nutrition can affect hearing. The ear is the most energy-hungry organ in the body. It has the greatest number of blood vessels and the highest metabolic rate of any organ and requires a constant supply of nourishing blood to keep it functioning properly. Cho-

133

lesterol may collect in the blood vessels inside the ear, clogging the access of blood and reducing hearing ability. A low-cholesterol diet therefore makes sense for hearing as well as for general health. Proper diet combined with exercise is even better.

A sensible diet also includes the vitamins and minerals essential to good health. Some experts believe, for example, that a zinc deficiency may contribute to progressive sensorineural deafness. Excessive salt intake, unhealthy anyway, may make a certain type of fluctuating inner-ear deafness worse.

When you take a plane trip, your ears may bother you, especially during descent. The pressure in the cabin changes, and your ears may feel "full" and even painful. The Eustachian tube has to open to allow the pressure on both sides of the eardrum—in the middle ear and in the outside environment—to equalize. If you yawn or swallow, you will notice the Eustachian tube "pop" as it opens and you will feel more comfortable. Chewing gum or sucking a hard candy makes you swallow and helps to open the Eustachian tube. Try not to fall asleep as the plane descends. You may not swallow frequently enough to keep the pressure equalized. If you have a stuffy nose you can take an over-the-counter, nonprescription antihistamine and use a nasal spray about an hour before the descent begins in order to clear the passages. If you have a bad head cold, don't fly. Your nose and the lining of the Eustachian tube swell and become more difficult to open, and ear damage may result.

This chapter seems to be full of do's and don'ts. This is because it is obviously much better to diminish the dangers and possibilities of permanent damage to your ears than to start a problem that will be with you for life.

Your hearing is one of your most precious possessions. Look after it.

APPENDIX

ORGANIZATIONS OF AND FOR THE HEARING-IMPAIRED
AND OTHER SOURCES OF HELP

Alexander Graham Bell Association for the Deaf, Inc.
3417 Volta Place NW
Washington, DC 20007
Membership organization focusing on speech education for hearing-impaired people. Oral Deaf Adult section and International Parent Organization. Publications and information.

Better Hearing Institute
P.O. Box 1840
Washington, DC 20013
Information about hearing loss and help available. Hearing Helpline.

Captioned Films for the Deaf
Modern Talking Picture Service, Inc.
5000 Park Street N
St. Petersburg, FL 33709
Free loans of captioned educational and entertainment films and videos.

Also contact:

National Audiovisual Center
U.S. General Services Administration
Washington, DC 20409

Walt Disney Company
Educational Media
500 S. Buena Vista Street
Burbank, CA 91521

Deafness Research Foundation
9 East 38th Street
New York, NY 10016
Supports research and provides grants for work on causes, treatment, and prevention of deafness.

IBM National Support Center for Persons with Disabilities
P.O. Box 2150
Atlanta, GA 30055
Information and help on how technology, especially computers, can improve the quality of life for the disabled person in school, home, and workplace.

National Association for Hearing and Speech Action
10801 Rockville Pike
Rockville, MD 20852
Consumer affiliate of the American Speech-Language-Hearing Association. Services and information on communicative disorders. NAHSA Helpline.

National Association of the Deaf
814 Thayer Avenue
Silver Spring, MD 20910
Consumer organization concerned with communication skills and legal and employment rights of deaf people. Information on total communication. Junior NAD. Publications.

National Captioning Institute
5203 Leesburg Pike
Falls Church, VA 22041
Provides closed captioning service for television networks

and other programs, cable, home entertainment video-cassettes, advertisers, and other organizations.

National Hearing Aid Society
Hearing Aid Helpline
20361 Middlebelt Road
Livonia, MI 48152
National Helpline helps answer questions about hearing loss and hearing aids.

National Information Center on Deafness
Gallaudet University
800 Florida Avenue NE
Washington, DC 20002
Provides information on deafness, hearing loss, and Gallaudet University.

National Theatre of the Deaf
The Hazel E. Stark Center
Chester, CT 06412
Artistic and professional development of deaf actors and actresses. Tours the United States and abroad.

New York League for the Hard of Hearing
71 West 23rd Street
New York, NY 10010
Rehabilitation agency for infants, children, and adults. Audiology, technical services, communications, psychological and social services, educational counseling and job placement, outreach, publications.

New York Society for the Deaf
817 Broadway
New York, NY 10003

Comprehensive services for deaf and deaf-blind persons. Use of sign language, lipreading, or whichever form of communication with which the client feels comfortable. Interpreter referral service. Sign language classes for hearing and deaf people.

Self Help for Hard of Hearing People, Inc.
7800 Wisconsin Avenue
Bethesda, MD 20814
Promotes awareness about and provides information on hearing loss, communication, assistive devices, alternative communication. Publications. *Operation SHHH:* program for educating schoolchildren on the damage to hearing by noise, featuring SHHHerman the Lion.

Telecommunications for the Deaf, Inc.
814 Thayer Avenue
Silver Spring, MD 20910
Special-interest organization supporting technology in the field of visual communication, especially TDDs.

HEARING EAR DOGS

Canine Companions for Independence
Executive Office
P.O. Box 446
Santa Rosa, CA 95402

Hearing Ear Dog Program
Executive Office
P.O. Box 213
West Boylston, MA 01583

Red Acre Farm Hearing Dog Center
109 Red Acre Road
P.O. Box 278
Stow, MA 01775

BIBLIOGRAPHY

NONFICTION

Arthur, Catherine. *My Sister's Silent World*. Chicago: Children's Press, 1979.

Bowe, Frank. *I'm Deaf Too*. Silver Spring, MD: National Association of the Deaf, 1973.

Butterworth, Rod R., and Mickey Flodin. *The Pocket Book of Signing*. New York: Putnam/Perigee, 1987.

Gannon, Jack. *Deaf Heritage; a Narrative History of Deaf America*. Silver Spring, MD: National Association of the Deaf, 1981.

Grant, Brian, ed. *The Quiet Ear: Deafness in Literature*. London: Faber and Faber, 1988.

Greenberg, Judith E. *What is the Sign for Friend?* New York: Franklin Watts, 1985.

Griffin, Betty F., ed. *Family to Family*. Washington, DC: A.G. Bell Association, 1980.

Groce, Nora E. *Everyone Here Spoke Sign Language*. Cambridge, MA: Harvard University Press, 1985. (Martha's Vineyard community)

Higgins, Paul C. *Outsiders in a Hearing World*. Beverley Hills and London: Sage, 1988.

Humphries, Tom, Carol Padden, and Terrence J. O'Rourke. *A Basic Course in American Sign Language*. Silver Spring, MD: T.J. Publications, 1980.

Lane, Harlan. *When the Mind Hears: A History of the Deaf*. New York: Random House, 1984.

Lane, Leonard. *The Gallaudet Survival Guide to Signing*. Washington, DC: Gallaudet University Press, 1987.

Levine, Edna S. *Lisa and her Soundless World*. New York: Human Sciences Press, 1974, 1984.

Padden, Carol, and Tom Humphries. *Deaf in America: Voices from a Culture*. Cambridge: Harvard University Press, 1988.

Rezen, Susan V. and Carl Hausman. *Coping with Hearing Loss*. New York: Dembner, 1985.

Schein, Jerome D. *Speaking the Language of Sign*. Garden City, NJ: Doubleday, 1984.

———— *At Home Among Strangers*. Washington, DC: Gallaudet University Press, 1989.

Walker, Lou Ann. *A Loss for Words*. New York: Harper and Row, 1986.

Ward, Brian. *The Ear and Hearing*. New York: Franklin Watts, 1981.

Wolf, Bernard. *Anna's Silent World*. Chicago: Children's Press, 1979.

FICTION

Corcoran, Barbara. *A Dance to Still Music*. New York: Atheneum, 1974.

Greenberg, Joanne. *In This Sign*. New York: Holt, Rhinehart and Winston, 1970.

Hodge, Lois L. *A Season of Change*. Washington, D.C.: Gallaudet University Press, 1987.

Levinson, Nancy S. *A World of Her Own*. New York: Harvey House, 1981.

Mango, Karin N. *Just for the Summer*. New York: Harper and Row, 1990.

Riskin, Mary. *Apple is my Sign*. Boston: Houghton Mifflin, 1981.

Rosen, Lillian. *Just Like Everybody Else*. New York: Harcourt, Brace, Jovanovich, 1981.

INDEX

DATE DUE